'This is a remarkable story of courage, faith and perseverance. It is a heart-rending account of what one family
went through – their brokenness, trials and difficulties.

'Their inspiring example encourages us all to keep
going through hard times, knowing that we are not on
our own.'
Pippa Gumbel

'Where is God when it hurts? Why doesn't He put right
our pain? In this overwhelming account of tragedy piled
upon tragedy, the slow erosion of human spirit is painfully exposed.

'Ironically, it is often precisely at the point of utter
despair that our awareness of God's existence is at its
sharpest. This awareness is not necessarily brought about
by the suffering, but because we are at our most receptive.

'This is an uplifting and inspirational story – undoubtedly reaffirming God's existence.'
Diane Louise Jordan

'A truly inspirational book.'
Lisa Potts

'The word "harrowing" comes to mind first of all and also
"brilliantly written". It is an amazing book but deeply
painful to read.

'It gives the most incredible insights into suffering. I believe everyone who reads this book will be deeply touched. It takes an enormous amount of courage to be as honest as Julie has been but oh, how wise it is and what a comfort it will be to so many people. Christians who go through these awful experiences don't just bounce, jump and shout with triumph, any more than the Lord did in the Garden of Gethsemane. That's why the book is so very valuable.'
Jennifer Rees Larcombe

'Julie and Georgie's story caused tears to flow down my cheeks, not with pity or sorrow, but rather of thankfulness and indebtedness – for our God's sustaining love and faithfulness throughout their many buffeting storms.'
Brian Gault

One Step
at a Time

A Story of Endurance
and Perseverance

Julie Sheldon
with Lucy Elphinstone

Hodder & Stoughton
LONDON SYDNEY AUCKLAND

Copyright © 2000 by Julie Sheldon and Lucy Elphinstone

First published in Great Britain in 2000

British Library Cataloguing in Publication Data

A record for this book is
available from the British Library

ISBN 0 340 74 623 8

Typeset by Hewer Text Ltd, Edinburgh
Printed and bound in Great Britain by
Clays Ltd, St Ives plc

Hodder & Stoughton Ltd
A Division of Hodder Headline
338 Euston Road
London NW1 3BH

This book is dedicated to all the little friends we made in hospital. Their young lives were brought to an end before they could take the next step: John H., Daisy T., Joe C., Olivia H. and another older friend, Geoffrey G.

We also dedicate the book to Ross and all families who continue to persevere and endure through the confusion that childhood cancer brings.

Acknowledgments

We gratefully acknowledge the following, extracts from which appear in this book:

Jenny Francis, *Belief Beyond Pain*, copyright © 1992 SPCK.

Henri Nouwen, *Adam, God's Beloved*, copyright © 1997 by Darton, Longman and Todd Ltd and Orbis Books, and used by permission of the publishers.

Andy Park, 'One Thing I Ask', copyright © Mercy/Vineyard Publishing. Administered by CopyCare, PO Box 77, Hailsham, BN27 3EF.

Christopher Reeve, *Still Me*, copyright © by Hutchinson and Crown Publishers Inc.

Martin Smith, 'Lord You Have My Heart', copyright © 1992 by Kingsway's Thankyou Music, PO Box 75, Eastbourne BN23 6NW. Used with permission.

1

. . . We know that suffering produces perseverance;
perseverance, character; and character, hope.

Romans 5:3–4

I was transfixed.

The crab scuttled across the sand and then waited, stock still. With eyes darting from side to side he began to dig. Expertly, fine grains were swept aside until the hole was just big enough to bury his back legs and shell. Again he shuddered to a halt, and waited. All at once, with the blink of an eye, he was gone, retracting his legs and claws in one swift movement.

A few seconds later the crab reappeared, just as a couple approached walking hand in hand along the beach. They were scuffing the sand with each step as their arms swung back and forth together, their gaze only for each other.

Little did they know that all the effort a few moments earlier from a small creature in his sand world below had been wasted. The pair's love walk along the beach had filled in the hole. The crab looked momentarily startled at the disappearance of his latest excavation, and then began to dig again.

I lost count how many times this spectacle was repeated. There seemed to be innumerable obstacles and hazards ruining the day's earthmoving, not least the incoming tide. But after each new earthquake the inhabitant would reappear, dust himself down and start all over again. What was it that kept him going? Why didn't he just roll over onto his shell, put his claws in the air, and give up?

I know how he must feel. During the past few years, it has seemed as if my world has kept crashing down no matter how many times I tried to rebuild it. In fact, rather than digging a hole to get *into*, I have been constantly grappling and clawing to get *out*. Through it all I have been trying to understand what it means to endure and persevere in difficult circumstances. An overriding temptation has been to 'roll over, give in and give up'! But something inside, very deep down inside, persists. Somehow, when all seems spent through the long enduring of a situation, when all physical, emotional and spiritual strength seems gone, there appears to be a tiny well of 'last resort' to urge you on to persevere. Sometimes I don't even *want* to dust myself down and start all over again, yet this minute spark of life, light, hope – whatever it is – flickers bravely and encourages perseverance.

Our younger daughter was diagnosed with a malignant brain tumour just after her tenth birthday. Following years of struggling with the after-effects of surgery, chemotherapy and radiotherapy, I asked her if she might like to write her own thoughts on endurance and perseverance. Late one night she appeared at our bedside clutching her notebook. She was trembling. The words she'd written were drawn from such a depth that it had shaken her. Falteringly she began to read, and as she did so, I saw that out of the heart and mind of a child God was giving me a little glimpse of understanding: how from the deep darkness and hazards of a hole, God may not always rescue us but will bring ways to enable us to survive within it – to endure and persevere. It is with Georgie's permission that the words she wrote are reproduced here:

Go on? Why yes, that's what is expected of me.

Be brave, you say? Why yes, that's what is expected of me. (And what I expect of myself.)

Yet why should I be brave? Who am I being brave for?

The days wear on. I feel as if I am in a vicious circle dream. No one really understands. Does it matter if I cry? Will I upset you? Another headache.

Cheer up, girl. (After all, that's what is expected of you.) I put on my mask again. 'Yes, I'm fine, thank you.' Inside everything is churning. I close my eyes and feel sick again. Just another day feeling . . . Words don't really describe the feeling.

The tears are locked in. I feel like a bottle of fizzy lemonade that has been violently shaken; longing to be opened to let the fizz come whizzing out. The lid must be screwed on too tightly. Shan't, can't . . . and now won't let the tears out.

More pain. Incredible pain. A sense of 'not quite being all there'. A new thought: should I just end it all? Today. Now. How?

Yet something keeps me from this. Something from within, deep down. A voice. It says,

'I love you, Georgie. You're special, Georgie. You are needed.'

I lie in bed looking at my big picture of Jesus the Shepherd with all the sheep around him. There is also a girl in the picture who is being led by Jesus, his arm around her shoulders. Mum always said the little girl was me. Standing on the other side of Jesus is a boy. He is trying to get Jesus's attention, but it seems as if he is saying,

'Wait a moment. I'm just spending some time with Georgie.'

That's it! That's the voice I hear deep down. It's Jesus saying,

'I love you, Georgie. You are special. I have a plan for you. Your life is precious to me.'

I know now why I keep going. Why I keep enduring. Why I try to persevere.

'You are special,' *he says.* 'You are special.'

Perhaps an understanding of how special we are in the sight of God would help us not to feel it was *he* who had pushed us down the hole in the first place!

2

Let us run with perseverance the race marked out for us. Let us fix our eyes on Jesus, the author and perfecter of our faith, who for the joy set before him endured the cross, scorning its shame, and sat down at the right hand of the throne of God. Consider him who endured such opposition from sinful men, so that you will not grow weary and lose heart.

Hebrews 12:1–3

Two weeks before our ten-year-old younger daughter became ill, I remember exclaiming to my husband Tom, 'I don't think I've ever been more happy than now!'

It was almost six years since I had recovered from a very long illness. During that time we had lived through redundancy, desperate financial problems and the near loss of our home. My book *Dancer Off Her Feet* had ended with the celebration of the 'In the Pink Party' on the first May Bank Holiday weekend, but on the Tuesday Tom was out of a job. Life was to become a hand-to-mouth existence.

But there was real blessing too, quite apart from the physical healing I'd received. I hadn't realised that because I had a book published life would then involve becoming a speaker. I had no training at all in public speaking although, as a dancer, I was used to being 'on stage'. How much easier it was to learn exact steps and feel that once mastered they would speak their own message. Talking from the heart was much more difficult. Suddenly numerous requests came in to speak at churches, women's groups, after dinners and lunches, *Alpha* groups, television, radio and for countless newspapers and magazines. It wasn't easy being up-front about experiences which had caused us all so much suffering; exciting perhaps, but I felt I needed to know *what* to say and *how* to say it. It felt like a skydiver must feel leaping out of a plane without a parachute. I had a faithful prayer team alongside but, even so, I often felt scared at the thought of the next speaking engagement.

After years of illness and weakness, I felt very vulnerable in front of a sea of curious faces. Having been a professional ballerina, perhaps I could have turned it into a 'performance', but I'd learnt to my cost that performing is about pretending there's no pain, about smiling and saying everything is just fine. The suffering of the past few years had stripped away my mask, my theatrical disguise, and brought me to acknowledge my need. I didn't want to become an exhibit or, worse, a celebrity, to get my sense of worth from being a speaker, a party turn. I got nervous, I made mistakes, and I longed for someone to teach me a few skills. I sought out people who were accomplished and experienced speakers and hoped they would take me under their wing and show me how to do it. But it never really happened. I carefully watched and listened and then, as a last resort, cried out to the Lord, 'How can I do this? I don't know how to be a speaker. The responsibility is too great. Help me!'

His reply came firm and deep in my spirit: 'I will show you *every* step of the way.'

So I stumbled on, learning to take longer, stronger steps each time. It was a privilege and a joy to describe the experiences recorded in *Dancer Off Her Feet*, but more than that it was a time of excitement and wonder, watching God heal and bring to himself those who were touched by this story. At the same time, there were years of family life to be made up, and any day spent travelling, preparing and speaking was a wrench. But I felt that as long as I had breath and people wanted to hear, I would tell of God's love and his power to heal today. My grandfather had a favourite saying: 'Stand aside, you bishops, and let the ordinary person catch a glimpse of the man from Galilee!' And in a way I wanted to take on that thought – making the message accessible to anyone who was trying to 'catch a glimpse'.

Time and again, I laid all this at God's feet, asking him when I should stop, change what I said, take time out. And once, when I felt weary of giving up yet another day to talk about him, he gave me a gentle reminder of why I should keep going.

I was waiting in the car, outside a girls' school, for the leader of the Christian Union to come out and show me where the lunchtime meeting was to be held. It had been a terrific rush to get there on time. Everything had gone wrong. It had been difficult getting the children off to school on time that morning, the phone had not stopped ringing when I was trying to get ready, I'd missed a quiet moment of prayer and preparation, the car decided to be all cold and fussy about starting, and to top it all I was having a bad hair day!

So as I sat waiting, relieved just to have arrived almost on time and in one piece, I let out a huge, impatient sigh. 'Why on *earth* am I doing this?'

I almost jumped out of my skin for I'm sure I actually heard an audible voice say, 'You are doing this for *me*. Remember what I did for *you*. I died for you.'

By the time the sixth former from the CU arrived, I'd dried my tears and felt raring to go. But it had shocked me deeply that I had been so careless and flippant in my approach to speaking to these young girls. It mattered that they heard about Jesus. It mattered that they too were told that he had died for them. That moment in the car has stayed with me and I remember it every time I go out to speak. Jesus paid such a huge price; I need only to be obedient and seek his will for every speaking engagement.

There wasn't just the miracle of my healing to talk about, though. The ripples had gone much wider. So many wonderful things were happening in our family and among our friends. My brother Nigel was so bowled over by what had happened to me that he gave his life to God. He sold his business and set up a Christian healing centre in the United States where he now exercises the gifts of the healing ministry, conducting workshops, lecturing, preaching and writing. He has received the Wittnauer International Humanitarian Award in New York for outstanding contribution to the community and is on the National Advisory Board of Christian Healing Ministries in Jacksonville under the leadership of Francis MacNutt.

The fact of my continuing good health and strength inevitably influenced many of those who were so affected by my distressing illness. Faith and hope poured into my family but, ironically, my husband Tom was the one whose faith appeared to change least. Having enormous reserves of natural strength and optimism, he had been more able to cope with the struggles of each day as they came during my illness. He was obviously full of thankfulness that the years of pain and heartache were over, but if they hadn't ceased, he might well have been able to plod on trusting, undramatically in the inscrutable wisdom of an unseen God. He accepted my healing with joy and relief but in itself it was not enough to move him beyond the comfort of his traditional Anglican faith. He was surprised, having seen at first hand the miracle of both my instant and my gradual healing, how his 'head hadn't connected to his heart'! He could *see* the physical miracle and rationalise it in his mind, but seemed unable to make the link with his faith.

In the summer of 1994 we were invited as a family on a Christian teaching holiday. Known as a house-party (or God Week, as our daughters affectionately call it) these holidays have since become an important part of our lives, and it was at this first one that God finally pierced the solid armour of Tom's self-reliance. A week before the house-party, he had asked God to clear away any prejudices and preconceived ideas and to give him an open heart to receive whatever God wanted for him.

Although reluctant about going on this house-party, Tom felt it would be rude and churlish to refuse the offer, especially as the week was being given as a gift. Halfway through the week, Tom was praying when suddenly he had a picture in his mind of a rolled-up scroll unfolding in front of his eyes. On the scroll, to his horror, was a list of his sins – none of which he could specifically read, but he was aware of the sheer *number* of sins he had committed. He was also struck by the fact that there were sins on this scroll that he didn't even know he had committed. As the list continued to unfold, he began to feel a terrible physical pain in his chest, especially in his heart, and it gradually dawned on him that what was standing between him and God on a personal level and as friend was his *sin*.

The following day he felt weighed down and depressed by this burden of guilt. Then someone mentioned to him that there was going to be a communion service that evening and it suddenly hit him that all he had to do was take his scroll – his list of sins – to the service. There he could lay it down at the foot of the cross, say sorry to God, and be released from this awful weight. In doing so he started what he describes as a wonderful love affair. Calm, dependable, unemotional Tom became on fire with his desire to tell others about the Christian faith. He went to Bible studies and meetings, eager to make up for 'lost time', and sought for every means to help those without hope in God to find the reality of his love. With both our daughters also knowing in a personal way God's deep love and care for them, I felt more happy than I can say!

There was icing on the cake too. My love of ballet was

still a strong force in my life, and to my pleasure both Mimi and Georgie had shown interest and talent. Mimi had sadly grown very tall and had not been able to go further. But Georgie had remained petite and dedicated, progressing through her exams with considerable success until she achieved her coveted goal – a place in the National Youth Ballet. Over 700 children audition for a place each year, and to our delight Georgie was one of the 160 children chosen in 1995. We were over the moon. She was given a part in the ballet *When We Were Very Young* based on the poems by A.A. Milne, and was also to dance the part of one of the poor Hummel family in *Little Women*. We all shared in the fairytale.

Not surprisingly, when Tom and I led the morning devotions on the house-party that summer, we were full of a sense of God's goodness and a desire to move closer to him in our thankfulness. It was here that I commented to Tom on the sheer happiness of my life. One particular morning sticks in my mind. It was the time of morning prayer for the house-party and Tom and I felt we should use a song by Martin Smith as the springboard for a deeper dedication of our lives:

> Lord, you have my heart
> And I will search for yours.
> Jesus, take my life and lead me on.

It was extraordinary how poignant and moving that song seemed. Little did we know how God would take that prayer and begin to answer it profoundly in just a few weeks.

We went off on our summer holiday, camping in

France, soon afterwards. It was a perfectly normal and very happy time with idyllic weather and masses of fun, beach activities and places to explore. The girls had lots of energy and we must have looked like any other normal British family enjoying themselves. In fact, we did wonder if we had had almost too much excitement as just at the end of the fortnight Georgie started to feel sick and headachy, and we regretted spending so much time in the bright sun. Still, as soon as we arrived back in England it was her tenth birthday so we were all caught up in the excitement of the preparations. Part of her present had been having her bedroom decorated just as she wanted it and this had been a big factor in making her feel that she was 'growing up' as she was allowed to choose the paint colours and curtains. Strangely though, despite all her friends coming round for a riotous and happy party, Georgie seemed irritable and exhausted, not herself at all. We thought it might be the aftermath of sunstroke or perhaps just overexcitement. We had no idea just how ill she was feeling underneath.

Then, quite out of the blue, Georgie started being violently sick first thing in the morning and unable to tolerate the morning light coming through her bedroom curtains. This had to be some sort of bug or virus. Somehow she struggled on with her weekly rehearsals at the Royal Academy of Dancing but she was clearly out of sorts. After two weeks the sickness was still troubling her although it passed off quickly as the day progressed. A visit to the GP (and her vomiting in his surgery) suggested it was 'just a virus', but I had a deeper suspicion. Perhaps only a mother or father would understand.

One afternoon, on returning from school, Georgie was

distressed because her piano lesson had gone very badly with a familiar piece she'd played so often being completely incomprehensible. I noticed, too, that her little face seemed to have 'dropped' on one side, making her smile lop-sided. An increasing dread in the pit of my stomach confirmed something more when her usually round and bold writing shrank to the size and shape of a demented ant! Her homework was illegible, and she didn't notice.

A referral note from the GP to the paediatrician at the local hospital introduced Georgie and made reference to how ill I, the mother, had been, this probably accounting for my over-anxiety about this child with 'just a virus'. Would they be kind enough to see her anyway? Just to keep me quiet, I suppose.

A young woman doctor came into the cubicle and to our amazement we found she, too, was called Georgie. Dr Georgie and little Georgie immediately got on and chatted easily. Much later on, we discovered that Dr Georgie had been studying brain tumours that very week in her medical textbooks. When Georgie told her what had been happening, she thought it was as if everything she'd recently read was being re-enacted through this ten-year-old child: the headaches, the sickness, the dislike of light, the diminished handwriting, the dropped smile, the pain in her eyes; it all added up to one thing. To be certain Dr Georgie ordered an immediate CT scan – and at that point I was just pleased I wasn't being fobbed off as a neurotic mother!

The wait outside the CT scanner passed fairly quickly. I was sad not to go in with Georgie and aimlessly flicked through magazines as the clock ticked by. The nurses brought her out finally and she appeared to be in good spirits. I could see the tall radiographer standing at the door of the scanner room so I smiled and went over to him.

'Everything all right?' I chirped hopefully.

Suddenly his eyes welled up with tears and he hurriedly looked away, stepping back inside his room. I lunged forward, noticing at the same time the nurses fussing over Georgie and saying they would take her back to the ward. A balloon of nausea erupted inside. Time stood still. All I could see was this man's sadness and I wanted to comfort him. With a jolt I realised he was crying because of Georgie.

'What's wrong? What have you found? Please tell me!'

'I'm sorry, I can't.' The brown eyes looked agonised. 'You'll have to wait to see the doctor again. I can't tell you anything.'

'Please, please,' I begged, my trembling hands gripping the cold metal of the door handle.

The radiographer composed himself on seeing my alarm and quietly offered, 'There is a little something there, but you must wait to see the doctor.'

Once, as a twelve-year-old girl, I had set the fire-alarm off during a dull afternoon at school. The same blind terror and panic I'd felt then now surged to the surface and, as before, I didn't know where to run, what to do or what to say. A kindly receptionist came to the rescue and offered me the telephone and a cup of tea. I phoned Tom at work and pleaded, through the tears, for him to come as quickly as he could. I couldn't say any more. The words wouldn't come.

There was a waiting room with comfy green chairs, a

sofa and a cheerful blue carpet. It's funny what you remember. The receptionist sat me down while we waited for the consultant to arrive. He was a charming, gentle man. Quietly – the words dropping into a silent, dark pool – he told me there was a little 'cyst' which had shown up on the scan. Looking back I am grateful to Dr Charles that he didn't use the words 'tumour', 'brain' and 'cancer'. I do remember, however, an overwhelming sense of sorrow for Georgie.

'Poor Georgie,' I kept on saying. 'Poor, poor Georgie.'

When Tom arrived, looking ashen, I ran to him and put my arms around him. When I could get out that a cyst had shown up on the scan, he seemed relieved.

'Oh! I thought for one awful moment she had died,' he replied.

3

On my bed I remember you; I think of you through the watches of the night. Because you are my help, I sing in the shadow of your wings. My soul clings to you; your right hand upholds me.

Psalm 63:6–8

Does lightning strike in the same place twice? The thudding sense of shock and disbelief we felt was compounded by a feeling of bewilderment, of sudden loss and familiar fear. Years of coping with pain and illness enabled Tom and me to put on a façade of calm as we listened to the arrangements for Georgie's urgent admission for brain surgery, but deep inside us both beat a pulse of terror. It was only out in the carpark that Tom's control almost broke and I caught a glimpse of how much he was hurting inside.

We were swept up into a vortex which had its own momentum. Georgie was to be admitted the very next morning into Great Ormond Street Hospital with a view to surgery to remove the tumour four days later. We only had a few hours to tell Mimi, pack a few clothes for Georgie and me, and make hurried, painful phonecalls to close family. It felt sadistic breaking the news to thirteen-year-old Mimi, smashing the happy world of her young hopes and dreams, filling her mind once more with all the uncertainties of her childhood.

'Life's never going to be the same again, is it, Mum?'

Panic was etched on her face and it was only the presence of Georgie herself, feeling too ill to summon any feelings except perhaps relief that soon she would be made better, which prevented our letting go. We all tried for each other's sake to keep the atmosphere calm, even trying to settle down finally to watch a film together, but Mimi felt so sick with anxiety that she kept running to the bathroom, and none of us really listened to a word. Sleep shunned us.

Being back in hospital was all too familiar to me. What ghosts must it have awakened for Tom and Mimi who had spent so many weeks and months of their lives already at hospital bedsides? The antiseptic smell, the swish of curtains and rattle of trolleys, the impossibly shiny floors, the drips and machines, the bustling, cheerful nurses, the hesitant tones of relatives, the Disney-brightness of children's art and cuddly toys . . . all the familiar sights and sensations settled on us like a shroud. With resolute cheerfulness we settled Georgie into her brightly decorated room, the murals and curtains reflecting the jungle theme of Parrot Ward. The room could also accommodate a parent and as we unpacked it didn't take long to personalise our surroundings, especially once we had put Georgie's pink duvet cover on the bed and tucked her in with her furry creatures and teddies.

Tom and Mimi left eventually to hold the fort back home. Clearly the news had spread rapidly and the phone rang constantly as soon as they entered the house, precipitating Tom to set up another number with a message line on the answering machine. This proved to be an invaluable lifeline to the prayers and support of friends and people at home and abroad. Many cards and gifts began to arrive. Such thought and empathy accompanied these generous parcels and it helped no end in the days ahead to focus on a new toy or a colourful, amusing card. The gifts of money, often anonymous, eased the burden of all the extra expenses that suddenly occurred, and made it possible to provide uplifting treats and even the idea for weekends away in the future. We were quickly overwhelmed by the depth of love and feeling people were expressing, and how they too were sharing with us in the shock and speed of the diagnosis.

The next few days went so slowly for Georgie and me and it was exhausting in the unnatural heat of the hospital. Different doctors, nurses, tests and checks passed before us with bewildering rapidity and much of my time was spent reassuring Georgie through the discomfort. A kind and clever 'play specialist' spent some time explaining the operation to Georgie, who took great delight in carrying out the procedures on a doll-patient, especially when she was allowed to give it an injection! I soon felt drained but at least I felt I was doing something positive, being actively involved in the fight against Georgie's illness. For Tom and Mimi it was harder. It's impossible to 'carry on as normal'. They both feared nothing would be normal for a very long time. Mimi went into school on the Monday but had to cope with the bizarre situation of several of her friends breaking down in tears and being sent to the school office. When she herself felt she could stand the strain no longer and presented herself at the office to recover, she was ticked off for getting in the way when so many girls were upset about poor Mimi Sheldon's sister.

'But I *am* Mimi Sheldon,' she protested.

It was the beginning of a deep-rooted anger in Mimi at the way people appropriated her grief and indulged their emotions, leaving her feeling comfortless and alone.

Now I was discovering first-hand how much more difficult it is to watch someone you love suffering than endure it yourself. On the day of the operation I would have given anything to have been able to go into the theatre instead of Georgie. Yet she was amazingly calm, despite the knowledge that a large piece of skull would have to be cut out to remove the tumour, which was the size of a golf ball and pressing heavily into her brain. It was explained to us that she might awake from the anaesthetic with paralysis, loss of speech, a fit, blind – it was an endless list of possibilities. The risks were clear. The operation would be long and delicate. We could only wait and pray.

Wednesday 27 September 1995 was one of the longest days of our lives. Saying goodbye to Georgie as she was wheeled down to the theatre, clutching a special Steiff bear named Petsy given to her by a recently bereaved friend, was desperate. She went down at nine fifteen in the morning and our friend Penny, who had been with us through all our trials with dystonia, joined Tom and me in the chapel of Great Ormond Street Hospital for prayer. How we longed for reassurance, hope and comfort. Instead I was confounded to feel an intense dread halfway through the morning. I was sure that something had gone wrong and no amount of anxious prayer brought a sense of peace.

More than three hours later, we watched Georgie's still body being lifted gently onto her bed. Sophisticated monitoring devices flickered and bleeped alarmingly; wires and tubes were attached to her chest and arms, and she looked so vulnerable surrounded by all this technology. A huge wound ran down one side of her head and grotesque wire clips were stapled into her skull. But she had survived! We could see her thin chest rise and fall almost imperceptibly. The doctors told us that technically there had been no problems in the removal of the tumour and that they hoped 90 per cent or even 100 per cent of the growth had been taken out. The question now was whether the operation had caused any brain damage. Would Georgie be able to move and speak?

Willing her to wake up, we held her hand and called her name. Her eyes fluttered. A nurse asked her to wiggle her toes. There was no response. My heart felt as if it would crumble. Again the nurse asked her to try. Then . . . a slight movement in her foot, and the tension in the room broke like glass. She wasn't paralysed. She could hear and understand us! With tears running down my cheeks I called her name again and at last her eyes opened.

'My head hurts,' her faint voice murmured.

She could talk. Georgie was with us. She had made it through. She had won her first battle.

The hours that followed led us along a rollercoaster of emotions. The initial euphoria was replaced by the gradual and sombre realisation of the long haul ahead of us. It would be several days before we knew the results of the analysis of the tumour, but it became clear that whether or not it was malignant, Georgie would probably have to undergo a painful and debilitating course of radiotherapy and possibly chemotherapy. We so much wanted to believe it was all over, but something deep inside told me that the fight was only just beginning.

Georgie appeared to recover remarkably from the operation. Within hours, she was propped up in bed sucking an iced lolly, and when the registrar asked her six hours later how she was feeling she replied politely, 'I'm feeling very much better today, thank you.'

But her courage hid the discomfort she was in, and the recognition of the same character traits as my own enabled me to see beyond the brave smile to the pain and fear beneath. Her own account of those first two days reveal what nurses and family perhaps never perceive:

Wednesday 27 September
  A lonely night.
  Mum has gone to the parents' room to sleep after much persuasion from the nurses. I wanted her to stay but I guess that was selfish of me.
  My head is really aching and my throat is dry and sore.
  The nurse in charge speaks very little English and doesn't understand when I start to cry. She carries on

*reading Mum's magazine and eating chocolate. I cry for
ten minutes under my breath. I don't want to wake up
the other children in the room but I really want Mum.*

*I start to shiver and finally decide to get this so-called
nurse's attention. She realises that I'm not just making
weird faces but am actually crying, and I tell her,
through great sobs, to get Mum.*

*She goes off for what seems like a lifetime and finally
comes back with Mum who is in her orange flowery
dressing-gown and nightie looking worried. She gives
me a reassuring kiss, tucks me in and makes me comfy.*

*That is all I remember of that first night after my big
operation.*

Georgie kept her struggles to herself. What we all saw was
the big smile and the bright eyes. By the next morning she
was getting up to use the bathroom, and although she had
a thumping headache, she was able to joke and laugh.
Unexpected pains set her back now and then over the next
few hours – she had a very sore cheek where the surgeon
had cut a jaw muscle, and a strange clicking sound in her
head where a piece of skull had been taken out and put
back again like a loose piece of jigsaw – but in the next few
days she appeared to make a remarkable recovery. My
sense of dread must have been misplaced. Her sense of
humour was undiminished and, when a friend came to
visit, she insisted on being photographed wearing an
oxygen mask to make it look more dramatic.

Lurking in the back of our minds, though, was Tuesday when we would get the results of the tests. There
seemed to be many types of tumours which could be
successfully treated, and we were praying so much that

this would be easily dealt with by radiotherapy and/or chemotherapy. All around us, in the other little children in the hospital, were reminders that the news is often not good. Young Marcus, who was admitted on the same day and into the same ward as Georgie, also had a brain tumour. We were really alarmed when he was rushed back into theatre a few days after his original operation as complications set in. Our two families shared in the anxiety and it was the beginning of an intense, but brief, friendship. Relationships such as this became very meaningful as only those in the same situation can understand the strain of sitting at a hospital bedside; we lived through each crisis with Marcus until our own threatened to engulf us.

Tuesday dawned and I waited in trepidation for our appointment with the consultant at 1.30 p.m. Tom was coming from the office and anxiously I scanned the swing-doors for his reassuring step. Dread had filled my stomach like lead and I didn't feel I could face the news, whatever it was, without him. Lunch-time came and I was desperate for him to arrive. At one o'clock I was startled by a gentle touch on my shoulder, 'Would you like to come in now, Mrs Sheldon?'

The nurse's sympathetic voice ushered me, alone and a bit cross at Tom's non-arrival, into the consultant's room. He didn't mince his words.

'I'm very sorry, Mrs Sheldon,' his words seemed to float in the air above my head, 'but the results show the tumour *is* malignant.'

I felt as if I'd lost my place in a script. I couldn't think of the right words. The cue was all wrong. To my horror, I heard myself laugh. He'd obviously made a mistake.

'Could you say that again?' I asked, shaking my head in a daze, glancing over to the nurse hoping she might be able somehow to change this man's words.

Patiently, slowly, as if he was speaking to a child, Mr Hayward explained that Georgie had a rare, malignant tumour which would not be easy to treat. Her chances were not good, but they would give her the 'belt and braces treatment'. Even so, the odds were no better than 25 per cent.

Tom then arrived just in time for one thirty to find me in a state of shock. I just couldn't believe this was happening to us. It felt like a film – or a nightmare. All that prayer, all that trusting and believing. All those years of suffering already paid. What had gone wrong? The questions couldn't even be considered just then. Gathering our devastated wits, we tried to listen while the neurosurgeon explained the probable course of treatment, tried to be brave, tried to be positive, tried not to cry. Tried to be strong.

You just don't tell your ten-year-old daughter that she might die. We gave Georgie whatever information she needed for the present and, in fact, she was feeling so much better than in the weeks preceding the operation that I really don't think she considered anything except a full recovery. It is a wonderful facility young children have, to live in the present and not worry about what the future may bring; part of their instinctive defence mechanism which we would do well to emulate. The treatment was unfortunate, she felt, but it wouldn't be long, would it, before she was completely well? It was a good thing that none of us had any idea of just what lay ahead.

4

*Consider it pure joy, my brothers, whenever you face
trials of many kinds, because you know that the testing
of your faith develops perseverance. Perseverance must
finish its work so that you may be mature and complete,
not lacking anything.*

James 1:2–4

Being shipwrecked must be like this, being washed up on
a strange beach, not safe on the mainland but on the shore
of a desert island. Survival would mean facing many
dangers and hardships. Rescue was not guaranteed. It
might be necessary to risk the perils of the sea once more.
Whatever was to come, we would need to dig deep and
row together to get through. Would we manage to keep
going? Could we endure the difficulties and persevere to
the end? For Georgie's sake we just had to.

Our emotions changed almost moment by moment. Home from hospital that Tuesday, we felt elated that Georgie was recovering so quickly from the operation. After two or three days' sleep it was hard to imagine that Georgie wouldn't be back to her normal self within days and we almost felt beguiled into thinking there must be some mistake and we would find that the worry was all over, there was no malignancy and no need for months of gruelling treatment.

If only. On the Friday Georgie had to have an MRI scan to check that the tumour had not spread elsewhere into her brain or spine. It was a traumatic and distressing process, being strapped down inside the tunnel of a machine for two hours, and Georgie got very claustro-phobic and upset, even though they had given her a sedative. After that we had to go back to the ward to get the eighteen metal clips taken out of her head, a procedure akin to medieval torture. Georgie's courage was amazing and the play specialist clever in her distractions. But when we got back home with Georgie, clutching a pot filled with her staples, she exclaimed, 'Thank goodness that's all over and I don't have to go back to hospital.'

What could we say to her? How we wished we didn't have to put her through so much more deliberate suffer-ing. But whatever it took, we were determined to do everything to help Georgie recover the vibrant life she had always enjoyed.

We weren't alone. Messages of love and support were pouring in every day, and the message line on the phone was a constant source of encouragement. In the darkest moments of fear and doubt, so often a word of love and faith would lift us up. Georgie's school-friends delivered boxes filled with presents and wonderful, creative, home-made cards, their own childish messages filled with life and hope. Our families were tireless in their practical help and at this stage God's presence felt very real. It wasn't always to be so.

Four days later we presented ourselves, taut with anxiety, to the consultant and registrar at Great Ormond Street Hospital to hear the results of the MRI scan. But the smiles on their faces said it all. There was no trace of the tumour having spread to Georgie's spine or elsewhere in her brain. Relief swamped us but it wasn't long before our joy had been tempered by their next piece of news. A difficult choice lay before us. We were asked if, in addition to the radiotherapy which was the standard treatment for malignant brain tumours, we would agree to Georgie entering a trial involving chemotherapy. Apparently at that stage they did not know whether che-motherapy actually increased the chances of recovery. Opting for the trial would mean that by random selection Georgie would either go into the control group and receive radiotherapy alone, or be a member of the group receiving radiotherapy with chemotherapy.

It was an agonising dilemma. Thoughts of rats and laboratories, guinea-pigs and experiments came to mind. No parent would want to deny their child any treat-ment which would increase their chance of survival, and it was made clear that the tumour was difficult to treat, being rare and in an unusual location. But a trial? Random choice? Maybe? Maybe not? The doctors left us under no illusion concerning the drawbacks of chemotherapy and radiation. But this seesaw of deci-sion-making was fraught with pros and cons. We thought we understood the drawbacks but no one can prepare you for the reality.

After days of searching for every piece of informed advice, both medical and spiritual, we felt we should consent to the trial and commit the 'random choice' to God. The uncertainty over which path we would take took its toll on us all, but after a week it was all finally agreed. Georgie would have chemotherapy for three months involving four three-day periods in hospital, followed immediately by thirty-three radiotherapy treatments which would last six weeks. Despite our natural apprehension, we did feel that we could rest in the certain knowledge that Georgie was under the best medical care and under the wing of a loving God who would be with us every step of the way. As a family we were able to speak freely about her illness and Georgie knew that it was cancer. The battle lines were drawn but we felt that it could be won, not least because we were blessed with a large army of friends and family who were constantly praying.

'I'm just going to take it one step at a time,' said Georgie.

The next step seemed like a stumble. Leaving the glorious late October sunshine behind, Georgie and I once again entered Great Ormond Street Hospital to prepare for the fitting of the Hickman line, the silicone rubber tube to take the chemotherapy drugs to save injecting constantly into the skin. It was meant to be in place for the three months of treatment but ended up staying for six.

It was an unpleasant procedure. In a half-hour operation the tube was tunnelled under the skin of her chest wall just under her arm, up into one of the veins in her neck and then with another incision in her neck down into the right atrium of her heart, leaving a six-inch length dangling from her chest. Back on the ward, Georgie was very distressed and in a lot of pain, particularly in her neck. Throughout the afternoon she drifted in and out of fitful, aching sleep but by the evening she was running a temperature. Through the anxious watches of the night I struggled again with the sense of guilt that we were putting her through all this extra pain. Realisation of the dangers of infection made me wonder whether we were doing the right thing. But the alternative carried even greater risks. We could only go forward.

When Tom came in to see her the next day, Georgie was very low.

'Today has been the worst day of my life,' she sobbed.

It's a good thing we don't know what the next day will bring, where the next step leads. In the months ahead we would come to see this as a relatively high point in the treacherous mountains and gullies we were to climb. The base camp of Everest is at quite a high altitude and the terrain preceding it arduous enough. Climbers getting that far can be fairly exhausted already. But experience of the exertion and hardships ahead causes previous discomforts to pale into insignificance.

The side effects of chemotherapy are well known. In the previous three years an anti-nausea drug had been developed which could be given before and after the treatment (it costs a great deal in liquid form so obviously they hope you can swallow the pill!). Georgie rallied a little the next day and a slight improvement in her temperature coupled with satisfactory renal tests meant that she was able to start the chemotherapy – and swallow the pill. The drugs take all day to administer and by the afternoon Georgie had become quite a dab hand at pulling her trolley with all its pumps, pipes and plastic bags round the ward with her. We played the computer Nintendo game enthusiastically and then graduated to snooker. The play specialist offered painting, crafts and more doll-injecting, and the hospital schoolteacher was not far behind. We were quickly realising that Great Ormond Street Hospital is a very special place with extremely dedicated staff and volunteers. Meanwhile, as the medical profession gave their finest expertise, family and friends throughout the world assembled their armoury to do battle. Even in Australia, one of my twin three-year-old nieces went up to the vicar after their Sunday service and said to him: 'Jesus, could you make my cousin Georgie better, please?'

The vicar replied, 'But, my dear, I'm not Jesus.'

'Ah well,' she answered, 'that doesn't matter. You'll do!'

The calm before the storm. The still moment before the fight is joined when blessings are remembered, prayers said, muscles tensed and breath deeply drawn. In so short a time we were caught up in the heat of combat . . . We went to choose a wig for Georgie in anticipation of the inevitable hair loss, and in pugnacious mood we urged her to get one straight blond one and one outrageous number, a green punk, perhaps . . . Then we bought several baseball caps and other people quickly cottoned on to the idea so that within a few weeks Georgie had a fantastic collection of about eighty amazing items. In America my brother Nigel had encouraged his friends to send 'The New York Giants' and 'The Dallas Cowboys' baseball caps. Once, when he went to the post office to send one of these parcels, after declaring its contents on the green customs declaration form, the American postmaster got chatting to Nigel.

'I see you're sending four baseball caps to England. I collect them too.'

Nigel began to explain how his niece would soon be needing them to cover her bald head and this man was so moved by her story that he asked Nigel if he might send 'the little gal in England' some caps from his own collection! My other brother Alec and sister Annie found a second-hand snooker table in very good condition and arranged for it to be delivered to our home. Mimi and Georgie enjoyed happy games together 'potting the black', and there was joy and laughter even as the dark clouds gathered.

5

See, I have refined you, though not as silver;
I have tested you in the furnace of affliction.
Isaiah 48:10

Sickness, aching limbs, ulcers, tummy pain and headaches.
This was the expected litany of side effects and Georgie
wasn't spared. What we weren't prepared for, though, was
an immediate infection in the Hickman line site and a
plunge in Georgie's blood count below the critical level
where a blood transfusion is needed. In the midst of this, a
group of twenty-five people were meeting at our house for
an *Alpha* course, a nationwide series of talks and discus-
sions on the Christian faith. It was difficult for all of us to
concentrate when Georgie was lying upstairs dizzy and
weak, waiting to be taken into hospital and in the interval
between talks, Tom and two friends prayed for her.

In the afternoon I took her to Maidstone Hospital for a blood test so that the right type of blood could be matched and sent down from London, and then we returned home to await the summons to go in overnight for the six-hour transfusion. The phone call came, but the nurse's perplexed voice told us that, to their surprise, the blood count had gone up from 7.9 that morning to 11.8, almost unheard of during chemotherapy, and a transfusion would not be necessary. She was mystified as to what had happened and even ran the test another four times to be certain, but to us it was confirmation that God's hand was on Georgie's situation and that he did hear our prayers. It was as if God was giving us hope and encouragement to draw upon in the future. In the months to come we were to need these reminders to keep a positive attitude and to stop us slipping into despair.

Each day brought its fresh challenges and hurdles, interspersed with moments of brightness. We all wanted Georgie to have as normal a life as possible, but it wasn't easy with her unable to attend school and missing all her friends and their happy companionship. Friends and family rallied round to amuse and entertain her during the long days: Jill came to bake bread or paint if Georgie had the energy; Mary and Alexandra also offered their artistic skills or sat with her snugly watching a film if she was too weak to sit up for long. And it was alarming how quickly she lost strength. Within two weeks of starting the chemotherapy, Georgie was needing a wheelchair to go outside for any distance, and something which should have been a great treat – going shopping – became a formidable challenge. Her school-friends remained in close contact and patiently waited until such times as she wasn't so open to infection.

Nevertheless, before her next dose of chemotherapy, I wanted to take her to Brighton for the day, ostensibly to go and have a change of scene, some sea air and visit the pier, but more particularly because a conference was being held there and the speaker that day was a man with an amazing ministry of healing and miracles, Mahesh Chavda.

I had read his book, *Only Love Can Make a Miracle* just a few months before and had been really excited and moved by its incredible accounts of healing. Mahesh Chavda grew up in Mombasa, Kenya, the son of a prominent Hindu teacher. He became disillusioned with the Hindu faith and turned to the Bible. One night God spoke to him in a powerful vision of the Spirit, and he gave his life to Christ. As a graduate student in Texas, he was filled with the power of the Holy Spirit, and almost despite himself an extraordinary ministry developed. When we learnt he was to be speaking and ministering at the Brighton Conference for Revival and Renewal in November, I just *knew* I had to be there.

On the Wednesday I had been down to Brighton with my sister-in-law, Polly, and was thrilled and amazed by this man's ministry. His faith, love and authority shone out. At the end of the meeting I managed to get a moment with Mahesh in the midst of the seething throng of people seeking his ministry, and asked him if he would pray for Georgie. Fixing his eyes steadily on my face, he told me to bring her the next day if I possibly could, or if not to bring a photograph and a garment.

It took a little persuasion to get Georgie to agree to

come to Brighton the next day. She couldn't go out without a wheelchair and she hated the idea of the attention she might attract, and people swooping to lay hands on her. The promise of a visit to the slot machines lured her to the seafront at last, and after candy floss and losing masses of twopences in the amusement arcade, we agreed to abandon the wheelchair in the conference cloakroom and then felt a bit more ready to face a renewal meeting!

What happened next was so dramatic that it would be impossible to describe. I have asked a close friend who was there with me to give her account of what she saw:

Thursday 9 November was a very big day. On Wednesday Julie told me that she had been to hear Mahesh Chavda and that he had asked her to bring Georgie or a garment and photo of her. Julie had been greatly blessed by him and managed to persuade Georgie to come down the next day.

On the Thursday morning, after his talk, Mahesh called all the pastors forward for prayer ministry. My husband, a minister, went forward and we were prayed for together. Amazingly Mahesh also had a word of knowledge which I responded to, so making a connection with Mahesh which was to prove so important for Georgie later. It was like the Lord was fitting together a jigsaw puzzle.

As we finished being prayed for, we saw a crowd gathered around Mahesh and realised that Julie and Georgie weren't there. I caught sight of Georgie sitting on a tiered seat at the back of the auditorium with her Aunt Polly while at the front Julie stood waiting for a gap in the crowd and a chance to talk with Mahesh. It seemed a bit like the story of the crippled man let down through the roof by his friends to see Jesus. Georgie just had to reach him but when I encouraged her to come with me she didn't want. to. Taking God's authority under my breath, I put out my hand and said, 'Come on, Georgie, we'll do this together.'

Meanwhile my husband was trying desperately to manoeuvre Julie through the crowd. The crush was immense and I almost despaired of being able to get through. Time seemed to have slurred into slow motion, and I could hear Mahesh saying, 'I'm afraid you'll have to come back tonight. I can't pray for all of you now.'

In desperation I cried out, 'No, please! This is so important!'

His eyes scanned the sea of faces quickly and then rested on mine. Recognition flashed across his face and in seconds he was there, standing in front of us. It had been such a battle to get to this point that I burst into tears on my husband's shoulder.

I was dimly aware of the loudspeakers in the background asking everyone to clear the building in five minutes. But my eyes were on Mahesh as he prayed over Julie and Georgie in the name of Jesus. Like two ballerinas both of them fell gracefully to the ground at exactly the same moment. Georgie lay completely still as if she were unconscious but Julie was weeping silently, eyes shut and unaware. I went and knelt by Julie and as I did so I heard Mahesh pray in a voice full of strength and assurance against the cancer and the tumour. Then he prophesied that Georgie would be *used to heal the nations and that she would have a powerful ministry to tell people about Jesus.*

I thought of the many ministries which were birthed in pain and released in healing. The sense of love, joy and relief around us just couldn't be described, but all of us knew that something amazing had happened. As we travelled back to the hotel in the taxi I told Georgie what Mahesh had said and she replied, 'I'm so full of the Holy Spirit there isn't any room left for the bad cells.'

We went back to the hotel room and cried.

What a difference twenty-four hours can make. Georgie had her next infusion of chemo the following day but in the evening her Hickman line seemed to be 'tracking', which is when the infection seems to be moving up the tube, so it was straight back into Maidstone Hospital. A blood test showed that her platelet count was very low which leaves the patient prone to bleeding, and suddenly her gums started to ooze with blood. She was also severely neutropenic, meaning she had a very low white cell count and was extremely open to infection. The hospital put Georgie on intravenous antibiotics but she had an allergic reaction and an awful night with terrible itching and delirium.

All this just hours after dramatic prayer for healing! It was difficult not to feel confused and dismayed, but we all tried to rally our defences and hold on to what we felt we had received. The next day the infection seemed to be coming under control but her white blood cell count was still zero and infection was a constant worry. Tom and Mimi were incredible at keeping our spirits up. That evening we left Mimi with Georgie while we went to the staff canteen to grab some food, only to come back and find they were pulling handfuls of hair from Georgie's head. It wouldn't be long now before she would be completely bald and in some ways that might be easier than waking each morning to a pillow full of hair.

It was a blow to learn that her blood count had fallen even further and she had to be given a blood transfusion, but after that she rallied a little and we hoped that she might soon be allowed out of hospital, hopefully well enough to have another major dose of chemo at Great Ormond Street the following week. She was allowed out a week later but was so weak that she found even walking to the bathroom a great effort.

Messages continued to pour in on the phone line, and one friend said she had a picture of all our friends praying like an orchestra. Not all the instruments were playing at the same time, but as we all kept our eyes fixed on the conductor he would show each one of us when it was our turn to play. This image really freed us from the overwhelming sense of responsibility and burden to pray and made us see that everyone could contribute at different times without having to feel that they needed to be praying constantly. But our eyes had to be fixed on Jesus.

We were learning more and more to take a day at a time. The anxiety of these days was suddenly lifted by a dramatic improvement in Georgie's condition, and we leapt at the chance to spend a family day together, just like old times. The late autumn sun glowed warmly on Brighton once more and we played the machines on the pier, ate doughnuts, went to the sea-life centre and generally had a lot of fun. It was a tonic for us all. On one of the stalls, Mimi and Georgie won a couple of huge stuffed leopards. We were a normal family again. Except one little girl had lost nearly all her hair. One little girl was weak, pale and in pain. But the essential Georgie was still there – in her sparkle, her joy and her humour. More than anything we prayed that that would never be taken away.

6

Therefore we do not lose heart. Though outwardly we are wasting away . . .

2 Corinthians 4:16

It's always hard to feel you're missing out, but for Georgie, and to a great extent Mimi too, life seemed to be happening elsewhere. The girls' friends continued with their relationships and their parties, their schoolwork and hobbies, but someone had pressed the 'pause' button in our lives. Some of the time Mimi and Georgie longed to take part in all this, but often I think it all seemed so pointless and superficial to them. One thing, though, mattered a great deal to Georgie, and it must have been very hard to see it slipping from her grasp.

She had always dreamt of being a ballerina. After years of dedication and effort, she had already climbed some difficult steps towards her goal. At first we were just terribly disappointed to miss the rehearsals and the performance of the National Youth Ballet but gradually, as the effects of the treatment took hold, we began to realise that the loss might be far greater than we had imagined.

Georgie was feeling very ill on the night of the gala at Sadler's Wells and so we had to make do with a video recording of the performance, tucked up on the sofa. I was concerned at how upsetting it might be for her to see what might have been, but her face, bright-eyed and pale, betrayed none of her inner pain. Before the start of the ballet, the National Appeals Director of Barnado's, the charity for which the gala was held, came onto the stage to give a presentation. Our hearts missed a beat as he spoke:

> Tonight is about dreams and magic. But on a slightly sad note, I'd like to tell you, if I may, about a young girl whose dream will not come true this evening. I'd like you to think of Georgina Sheldon who should have, this evening, been performing in *When We Were Very Young* and *Little Women*, but unfortunately she had to go to hospital recently, where I'm pleased to tell you she had a successful operation. But I know that when the cast performs these ballets you will think of her and join in the company's best wishes for her speedy recovery.

Georgie's delicate face was flushed now and tears shone in her eyes. Those kind words meant so much to us all, but nothing could fully restore the loss of greater dreams than just that night's. We watched as other little girls danced their hearts out on the stage. It was a beautiful, professional performance, but completely heart-wrenching when a small voice from the sofa exclaimed, 'There! That's me! That should have been me . . . Did you see me, Dad and Mum?'

A few days later, a lacy pink ballerina Get Well card arrived through the post and we were overwhelmed to find inside the signatures of Darcey Bussell and many of the Royal Ballet principals. This meant a great deal to Georgie and lifted her spirits a little after the big disappointment of missing the performance at Sadler's Wells.

Meanwhile the chemotherapy treatment dominated our lives. Four major doses were to be administered at Great Ormond Street Hospital, necessitating a three- or four-day stay, and these were to be interspersed with 'top-up' doses at the local Maidstone Hospital which required daily travel. I remember early on in the diagnosis, the doctor had remarked to Tom and me that 'one of you will have to give up work and be available during all the treatment'. It seemed obvious, but *of course* I would be available. It was an exhausting regime for all of us – for Georgie suffering such discomfort and sickness on endless journeys, for Tom and Mimi struggling to visit amidst their own work and commitments, and for me, sitting constantly at bedsides, trying to encourage and reassure. Without the unfailing support of friends, family and often complete strangers, we would never have managed.

It was a huge relief, for example, to be put in touch with a wonderful lady called Peggy Wood who had set up a charity to drive sick children from Kent to the London hospitals, and soon Georgie and I were travelling in style in a comfortable ambulance which enabled her to lie down and rest after the treatment which made her feel so ill. Peggy herself had a grandson who had had leukaemia as a two-year-old and this gave her the determination and sensitivity to make a difference to the lives of similar children. Sometimes the ambulance called to pick up other children as well, and we formed deep friendships with the other families locked in the battle against cancer.

A particularly special bond formed between Georgie and a little boy called Ross as they travelled to London together thirty-three times for the radiotherapy treatments. Often one or other of them felt too ill to sit up in the ambulance and they would frequently end up lying one each end of the stretcher. They have given each other such support through all the hopes and setbacks and, in their young lives, have a link from this experience, the depth of which is very moving to see. It was good to have someone who *really* understood. They shared jokes about the doctors and nurses, planned exotic outings for when they felt better, and instinctively knew when to be quiet and pass the sick bowl!

Whereas for us mums it was like being on a rollercoaster. One day Georgie would be feeling a little better, go to a pottery class at school, attend a friend's birthday party or go out to the ballet in Sevenoaks; the next she would crash completely, needing help to get dressed, and be able only to crawl from her bed to the sofa. Chronic stomach pains turned many nights into torments and at the beginning of December her temperature began to climb again and her colour drained, indicating infection and a perilously low blood count. Snow covered the garden and it was a struggle to get the car dug out and

Georgie into Maidstone Hospital once more. A blood transfusion and antibiotics were inevitable as her frail body tried to fight back, and this time the infection seemed to be proving the stronger. Her temperature soared, and pain and nightmares robbed her of the chance to recuperate through sleep. Anxious hours turned into days, an endless succession of nurses coming to take her temperature, fix up drips and take blood. Eventually, as the early snow began to melt and a watery sun shone through the hospital window, the fever lifted and Georgie's brave smile returned.

It must have been so hard for Mimi. In the midst of all this, she was trying to cope with revision, exams and school concerts, all in a world which no longer really made sense and didn't have time for her. She was always so loving to her sister but, although she never articulated it, there were clearly times of anger and deep unhappiness. In the middle of all this she had a viral tummy bug followed by a heavy cold, but instead of a fuss being made and lots of attention and comfort, she had to be banished to her room in case she spread the infection to her sister. She was only thirteen herself and yet in many ways she had to act like an adult and, in a way, did grow into a maturity and faith far beyond her years. But at a price. Recently she wrote down how she felt during those early months.

I suppose part of the reason I've felt so angry all these years is because I'm a 'hormonal teenager' as my dad likes to put it! But I think a lot of my anger chunk comes from the fact that I've had to live on the edge, with my mum being seriously ill for four years and then, just when life seemed to settle down, my sister was found to have a malignant brain tumour.

The night I was told that Georgie had a 'growth' in her brain was surreally horrific. We were trying to be cheerful by watching a film but I had to keep on running to the toilet as I felt literally sick with nerves.

At this point we naively had no idea it could be cancer, but even at the age of thirteen I knew that the situation was deadly serious. I remember saying to Mum, 'Life isn't going to be the same, is it?'

A few weeks later a nurse from Great Ormond Street came to visit us. She took me aside for 'a little chat' but I was hardly in the mood for polite conversation. I hadn't eaten properly over the previous couple of weeks and at this point I was unable to cry, so I came straight to the point that everyone else was avoiding.

'She won't die, will she?'

I was fully expecting a lavish, cuddly reassurance that Georgie was going to be fine, but instead my blatant question was matched by an equally pertinent answer.

'Well, we'll do our best, of course. But her chances are around 50/50.'

Oh my God. How are we going to get through this? I can't cope. Help me, someone. Help me, God!

You discover later on that you do cope. There is no other choice. The only way I found I could survive was to take five minutes at a time and then, much later on, to move on to a day at a time. When suffering consumes your life and everything revolves around it, living really does take on a new perspective. You can't trust anyone anymore. No one can actually help you, and their polite *but often insincere offers of help are impractical and useless.*

All this anger that was boiling up inside me became a big deal to me. Eventually I made a list of all the incidents which had caused me to become constricted and 'hunched' by anger. These ranged from friends being unable to cope with my family situation, to stupid, childish comments from adults who think they're 'bonding with the sister' by saying things like, 'I know how you must feel,' and 'You must get so jealous of all the get-well gifts Georgie has received.'

Just how shallow did they think I was? As if a few presents were my greatest worry. I wish! It was so much more than that. I wasn't a jealous sibling. I had to grow up fast and almost become Georgie's third parent.

It sounds bad, I expect, but I found the Christians were the worst! They were always trying to bring God into the reason behind Georgie's cancer. Why couldn't they realise that the two were quite separate – the good and the evil – and that there was no way God had caused a little girl to go through all that pain.

The anger often reached boiling-point and I was convinced that at any moment I might explode. One fear was that I might shout out a string of uncontrollable, abusive words and then be classed as 'insane'. But I wasn't insane, just insanely angry. I even had dreams about standing up in morning assembly, in front of the whole school, and letting them know how much some of them had hurt me with their words, probably without even knowing it.

Now I've tried very hard to forgive those on my 'list' although sometimes I still have trouble controlling my anger. *You might imagine me to be some sort of loud-mouthed rebel but I'm not! It's on the inside that commotion originates, festers and has to be got rid of in some way.*

That way has to be God.

7

My flesh and my heart may fail but God is the strength of my heart and my portion for ever.

Psalm 73:26

Christmas, the festive season. Happy Christmas. Merry Christmas. The pressure to be jolly at this time of year is immense. And yet, of course, for so many people the cheerful greetings and broad smiles are such an effort and often disguise accentuated heartache or unusual stress. With Georgie so unwell, we appreciated afresh the plight of those who do suffer at Christmas and long to be free from their pain to enjoy a truly happy time. The disparity between our expectations for Christmas and the reality of our experience can make us despondent and depressed. Not only our health but our joy has been stolen. Such regrets only intensify our situations, we know, but the subtle seduction by self-pity can take us unaware. We longed to spend Christmas all together as a family in our own home, but we feared that even that would be snatched from us, and it became a particular request on the telephone prayer line that Georgie would overcome her infections, fever and low blood count sufficiently to allow us at least Christmas Day together.

I suppose we shouldn't be surprised when prayer is answered favourably but we could scarcely believe it when Georgie's temperature suddenly returned to normal on Christmas Eve and all at once we contemplated the wonderful prospect of a family Christmas all together. Dreams can't be big and they can't be far away when you are living with cancer. Strength and peace for the next step, that was what we were learning to seek. That Christmas really was a blessing and for a few short hours we lived and laughed as if nothing was wrong. As Georgie opened her stocking she wrote on the misted window, 'I'M SO HAPPY' and that really summed up the day for her. She had the honour of lighting the candle on the Christmas tree at church and even managed to have a go on the rollerblades her grandmother had optimistically given her. One hundred and twenty-four people telephoned over Christmas to say that they were praying for us, and it astounded us all just *how* happy we could be in the midst of illness. You really do appreciate these little oases of calm and become 'thankful for small mercies'.

Christmas Day was all the more precious for the onslaught which returned on Boxing Day. Nosebleeds greeted the morning and inevitably Georgie had to be taken back into hospital for a blood and platelet transfusion. She returned home the next day only to be rushed almost straight back into hospital again as her temperature rose hour by hour. Three days of antibiotics and more transfusions followed until she was let out once more into a frosty New Year's Eve morning. But by the afternoon her temperature was rising again and at ten o'clock at night we had to get her out of her warm bed, bundle her into a cold car and return to hospital. Not a crisis in itself but when there has been little sleep for days these small things can be the final straw.

A couple of bottles of bubbly comprised our New Year celebrations. Tom's parents popped in for a visit and had to don aprons and gloves in order not to spread any infection. We must have looked quite a sight but, as always, felt we could make a party out of a crisis! Inevitably you keep meeting up with parents of other children with cancer, and we saw in 1996 alongside two other families whose little children have sadly since died. The nurses too tried to bring a festive air to the ward, and one nurse secretly smuggled in her two kittens for Georgie to play with. This sowed the seeds of the idea for Georgie to have a pet of her own.

The last big dose of chemotherapy was scheduled for 3 January in Great Ormond Street but we desperately hoped that Georgie and I might be able to spend a day or two at home to allow Georgie to build up her strength a little. No chance. We came out of Maidstone Hospital on 2 January and had to go up to London the very next morning, with Georgie suffering from a lot of sickness, muscle and tummy pains, and aching in her head and jaw. Add to that the lack of sleep and there was no doubt she felt generally rotten. People asked us how we coped and we replied it was only with a lot of practical and prayer support, by taking one step at a time, and with the knowledge that we were trusting a God *'who girds me with strength and makes my way safe.' Psalm 18:32.*

The last dose of chemotherapy was the worst in terms of Georgie's reaction to the drugs and she was very sick. Nevertheless it was wonderful to leave that stage of the treatment behind and to think that we could now move on to the next. It seemed a bit like competing in a pentathlon: one round, one skill perfected; the next probably requiring completely different abilities, but the whole event demanding huge stamina and endurance. And at the centre of the arena it appeared there was one frail little girl whose only strength was that she loved Jesus – until you realised that, like an athlete, a vast support team was always by her side and far away others who loved her never gave up their spiritual battle on her behalf. In truth, everything which happened to Georgie happened to us all, our immediate family being gathered as if around a huge blazing fire which warmed us with its flames of love.

At least, that's how it often felt in the early days. The time was coming, though, when we would feel that the fire had all but died and that we stood alone and cold in the dark. And yet we were to learn that even when a fire appears dead, glowing embers keep its heart alive, and a breath of wind and a tiny piece of kindling can restore the blaze.

It was now bleak midwinter. Raw winds and driving sleet, numbed hands and depressed spirits. Georgie's blood count fell and she needed yet another transfusion. Infection was a constant threat. But no time for recuperation. Cancer gives no rest and takes no prisoners.

Immediately we were in the throes of discussing the radiotherapy which was to take more than two months.

The plan was first to make a plaster of Paris mask for her face and the back of her head. This would then provide the mould for the plastic mask which would be intricately and carefully marked with lines for the radiographer to direct the rays on precisely the site of the tumour, and Georgie would have to wear this mask for all her treatments.

What a messy procedure, having strips of wet plaster of Paris draped all over your face, leaving just a small breathing hole for your mouth, and then having to sit still while the plaster hardens. Georgie was amazingly brave and calm and somehow managed to smile throughout the process of the plaster setting so that the radiographer said she would have to smile for all of her thirty-three treatments! She then had to go for several planning sessions and simulated X-rays.

Getting the mask exactly right was a highly complex and delicate operation and when Georgie had the simulated X-rays, she was bolted face down in the mask for a long time while the radiographer struggled to adjust the markings to pinpoint accuracy. With two clamps holding her head rigidly in place, and only a tiny hole to breathe through, she became very claustrophobic and distressed, and the prospect of thirty-three of these sessions – one every weekday – made her very upset. After a week of preparations, when we thought that at last everything must be in order, it was decided that the lead blocks to shield her eyes and mouth were not correct and needed adjusting. Then, the next day, when the cameras were finally meant to roll, the radiographer was unhappy with the lining up of the head and spine which she found was 0.5 cm out, and Georgie was again left lying for half an hour face down in the mask while six technicians and radiographers debated what to do and made adjustments. This was very stressful for Georgie and she was left at the end with a terrible headache, dreading the traumatic experience which was to come.

Fear and anxiety now became our main enemies. The consultant saw Georgie and me together and spelt out all the possible and probable side effects from the radiotherapy. He didn't beat about the bush. I was horrified that Georgie was sitting there listening to all these frightening possibilities but to my immense relief, she didn't really seem to register them and simply said that during the interview all she could hear were the words, 'with God all things are possible'.

It was going to be extremely gruelling travelling to the Middlesex Hospital in London, often a six-hour round trip, every day for two months We were indebted to Peggy Wood's charity, the Kent Leukaemia and Cancer Equipment Fund (KLCEF), which provided the ambulance to and from the hospital every day, not least because it enabled Georgie to lie down after the treatments when she felt so sick and headachy. In the midst of all this, she also had to have another MRI scan to determine the effectiveness of the chemotherapy, but mercifully this one was not as distressing as the last.

The staff in the radiotherapy department were super. They were always cheerful and kind, and did their best to make a miserable ordeal as easy and bearable as possible. They needed their strength and good humour. Technically and emotionally it was a difficult procedure, and on one occasion two of the radiography machines broke down, which meant finding time for thirty other people to be treated on the two remaining machines. At one point the two broken machines were in pieces all over the floor with two technicians on their knees with manuals in their hands trying to put them back together again! Not an inspiring sight. Yet calm and reassurance were maintained and the staff were particularly good with the children and tried their best to keep them to their allotted times.

Georgie's own account best conveys the treatment:

In the Radiotherapy Room

I lie waiting. Waiting for the buzzing noise and then the nasty taste I get in my mouth.

It is lonely. Very lonely.

The blurred picture of Bambi on the floor and the 'Bare Necessities' song blaring from the tape recorder do not take away that fear deep down in my tummy.

I am being watched. I know that. But still it feels lonely.

'It won't take long. Only a few minutes.' But it feels too long.

I'm frightened.

My head is bolted in on both sides of the mask and I can't move. The tape stops. They won't come in now to turn it over because the treatment's not done yet. It would be too dangerous if they came in. Even a four-foot-wide lead apron wouldn't protect them from the light. But yet it's going into my spine and head. I'm only ten. I haven't lived my life yet so why is this happening to me? Why not someone bigger, older, stronger? I feel too weak for another day of treatment.

I can hear the machine moving nearer and the red beam hurts my eyes. A warm chill goes down my back and that terrible taste sets in. Nearly over. Then they'll come back all jolly as if nothing has happened and say how still I kept. It's all right for them. They haven't had to lie here thinking about whether the treatment is working. And if not, will I die?

My friends are at school. It will probably be maths. As they grumble about last night's homework or who should have won today's tennis match, I wonder if they could imagine anything worse than, 'Yuk, I've got soggy sandwiches for break again'?

I've had to grow up fast. Too fast. I want to be grumbling about homework and not have to know about all this 'grown-up stuff'.

'How did that go, Georgie?'

My 'I'm fine' mask goes on as I'm unbolted from the plastic treatment mask.

'Yeah, it was OK.'

On two occasions, Tom came with us in the ambulance to the Middlesex Hospital to see for himself how long and draining the day was. He described seeing Georgie being lain face down in the mask as it was bolted into its base as like watching someone being prepared for execution. He looked whiter than Georgie by the end of the fifteen minutes during which she had three lots of radiation of about ten seconds each. Georgie had by now lost all her hair and a great deal of weight. Naked from the waist up, her shoulder bones sticking out painfully, she clutched her tattered old teddy bear as she submitted to the radiation. It was dreadful to feel that we were pushing her into this treatment; that while we couldn't avoid the cancer we could have saved her from this extra suffering if it wasn't felt that this was her only chance of recovery. But on board the ambulance that week, being interviewed by Radio 4 for a programme on Peggy Wood, the founder of the Children's Ambulance and the KLCEF, Georgie talked about her experiences with her usual courage and enthusiasm. Being the spectator of suffering carries its own pain.

The world seemed out of joint in some ways during those weeks. Our close friend Julia Robson had died after a six-year battle with cancer and her death had filled us with a deep sadness. Julia had really loved life and had taught us to make the most of each moment. We were determined not to forget her perseverance and her joy in the midst of her suffering. It was her husband Tim who had given us the idea of a prayer line and he reckoned that they received about thirty thousand phone calls during her illness. We were discovering, like him, that we were never alone, never absent from the loving thoughts and prayers of friends, never beyond the gaze and touch of our heavenly Father.

Even when the IRA blew up Builder House, the London office of Tom's publishing venture. On the evening of 12 February, Tom came to pick us up at the Middlesex Hospital because we wanted to go and buy Georgie a fleece jacket as she was really beginning to feel the cold in her emaciated body.

'I know,' said Tom cheerfully as Georgie and I climbed wearily into the car. 'Let's go and park down at Builder House, hop on the tube, nip into the Marks and Spencer store at Canary Wharf and then go and have a drink.'

It seemed a good idea to make use of the free parking space and at the same time keep the walking for Georgie to the bare minimum. But just as we were turning down the road to the office, Tom suddenly remembered that Marks and Spencer at Canary Wharf only sold food and not clothes, so he made a last-minute detour to Lakeside shopping centre instead.

Our guardian angel must have been working overtime. Less than an hour after Tom changed direction, Builder House took the full force of a massive explosion and was completely gutted. Mercifully, as most of the staff had already left for home, only twenty people were still in the building when the bomb went off. No one was killed inside the office but nine were hurt including a cleaner who lost an eye. Although the timing for us was such that we might not have been caught in the blast, our car, parked in front of the office, would have been totally destroyed.

The Docklands bomb meant that in the following days there were several more bomb scares and road closures, making travelling in the ambulance through the grid-locked traffic of London even more exhausting. Georgie was feeling very sick and her low blood counts necessitated a nurse coming to the house to take blood tests three times a week. She had completely lost her appetite and was increasingly weak and lethargic. Although the radiographers tried to cheer her up by calling her Kate Moss, there was no escaping the fact that she was now just skin and bone.

Family times were greedily snatched in between the treatments. On one Saturday, with Georgie in a wheelchair and Mimi pushing, we careered round the shopping centre to get Tom kitted out with some new clothes and then finished up by seeing a film together. Those days were so precious. There were also moments when we were able to feel part of the movement of God's Holy Spirit through the land as we took part in the *Alpha* course in our home. Almost forty people came one evening a week for ten weeks to hear talks about 'The Meaning of Life', and we read in *The Times* that 250,000 people were participating in the *Alpha* courses that year. It was good for us to focus on the need for everyone to hear the message that God can heal hearts and spirits as well as bodies. Without his grace we knew we were lost completely.

Halfway through the treatment, Georgie had to change over onto her back so that the radiation could be given face upwards. This meant a new mask and no more radiation on her spine, but rays coming in both sides of her head and through the front of her face, meeting at the site of the tumour. The prayers during this time were for protection of her eyesight and that her skin would not be blistered and burnt in the red, raw way we had seen on so many poor children.

Although the skin behind her ears did become quite red and sore, it didn't actually break down into blisters. We noticed, however, that the tiredness became even more acute with this phase of the treatment and her back, which could hardly bear even the slightest touch, ached with constant pain. Very soon her throat became sore and her whole body seemed to be struggling under the burden of the attack from the radiation. We counted off each day by rewarding Georgie with a daily sticker to put on a chart for each of the thirty-three treatments. It helped to bring us nearer to the end of the treatment, and as the snowdrops and crocuses gave way to primroses and daffodils, our hope began to grow stronger, and Georgie was photographed proudly holding her completed chart.

Spirits were lifted further by a lovely mini-break in Brighton and a visit to the Royal Pavilion, after which we even managed to sit on the beach for half an hour without our coats on. When we got back home, a surprise awaited us in the form of a beautiful doll's-house from the Starlight Foundation, a charity which exists to make dreams come true for children with chronic illness, and our *Alpha* group completely disintegrated that evening as all the ladies disappeared upstairs to play with the doll's-house rather than talk about the subject of the evening, 'How Does God Guide Us?'!

The MRI and bone scans which had been done on Georgie showed results 'within normal limits', a relief as her legs had been wobbly and painful in the mornings. The consultant felt this could either be still the effects of one of the chemotherapy drugs or her brain swelling in the night, but he was optimistic that these side effects would pass. We waited with increasing anticipation, therefore, for the last of the radiation treatments, and the start, we hoped, of Georgie's full recovery. On 15 March we left the radiation department for the last time, relieved but not, perhaps, with any great sense of elation. Georgie was very, very sick. Ever since the day of the diagnosis we had had an immediate goal to focus on and a feeling that we were doing something positive and tangible to fight back against the cancer. Now the treatment was over, we felt suddenly unsure and exhausted. The question on everyone's lips was, 'What happens now?'

8

In all their affliction he was afflicted, and the angel of
his presence saved them: in his love and in his pity he
redeemed them; and he bare them, and carried
them . . .

Isaiah 63:9, AV

It was going to be a long haul. We had five follow-up
appointments with the various departments and consultants, the first being one month later, when Georgie was
to have the Hickman line removed, and then she was
scheduled to see the surgeon, the radiotherapy consultant,
the growth specialist and then have another MRI scan in
June. But we were warned repeatedly that the side effects
could continue for months or even years. We couldn't
dwell on that. One day at a time was sufficient for us to
think about. Could we find the strength and courage to

get through just the next few hours? At this stage we felt surprisingly low. It's a good thing we didn't know that the next few steps of our path were going to lead even further downwards.

The doctors had warned us that in about a month's time Georgie might have a sort of 'big sleep' where she might literally sleep for most of the day because of the effect of the radiation to the head. In fact, she seemed to go into this almost straight away, not waking up until midday and then feeling so tired that all she could do was watch videos. We rigged up a hammock in the sitting-room so that she could curl up comfortably, surrounded by teddies and blankets, and watch the TV. This might sound cosy, but in reality it was extremely frustrating for Georgie who had been longing for the treatment to finish so that she could do all the things she and Ross had been planning in those long painful months. Headaches, sickness, aching limbs, extreme tiredness and tummy pains dogged her days; frightening dreams haunted her nights. The bad pains in her arms and legs fuelled fears that the tumour had seeded down her spine, so we were called into Great Ormond Street earlier than planned for Georgie to have more check-ups and another MRI scan. The neurologist seemed very concerned about Georgie's condition but the oncologist was more upbeat. Afraid of false hopes, we didn't know who to believe.

Our immediate desire was to get the intrusive tube of the Hickman line removed and to get Georgie into a bath! It was scheduled to be taken out under general anaesthetic on 17 April and our alarm duly went at five o'clock in the morning in order to be at Great Ormond Street Hospital by eight. Having got there, Georgie had the usual pre-op checks and was found to have a temperature so the operation was abandoned. This was a big blow for Georgie who had psyched herself up for the operation, and the disappointment was compounded by the doctors' concern over her severe weight loss and the decision that she would have to have a nasal gastric tube inserted so that she could be fed artificially during the night. So instead of having one tube out, she came home with the knowledge of having to have another put in. This procedure, carried out the next day, was deeply unpleasant as you can imagine, and the morale of us all hit rock bottom. Georgie had to have the tube in constantly and the end of it was taped to her face during the day. She looked and felt completely rotten.

A full head and spine MRI scan, due two days later, filled us with dread, not just at what the outcome might be, but also for the scan itself which would involve two hours in the machine again. We decided that desperate times called for desperate measures and agreed to fast as well as pray for this ordeal. Dozens of friends and family joined us in the fast and we felt extraordinarily supported and calmed as we walked through the doors of the hospital. Georgie did feel quite panicky at one point in the scanner but when she came out she was smiling.

'I could hear singing, Mum!' she exclaimed. 'Lots of voices were singing that song, "Let there be love shared among us", and I'm sure it must have been the angels.'

The angels must have been there, for the results of the scan showed no recurrent local tumour mass, and we tentatively breathed a sigh of relief. There were, however, cystic changes on the left side of the brain which would need further investigation but did not seem to cause the consultant too much concern. We celebrated this small positive sign by giving Georgie a kitten. Born in the neighbouring village, he was the only white one of the litter, but what made him even more special was his golden halo and he immediately became her little angel and she christened him Jack. It was amazing how much this tiny scrap of fur lifted her spirits and we were to discover that young Jack would bring more healing to Georgie than many conventional treatments. He would lie very still on her lap and make a delightful 'chirruping' noise of pleasure and joined her in sleep at every chance. The sense of calm and love this little animal engendered certainly made her eyes shine again, and gave her something beyond herself to nurture and protect; in that giving she found joy.

May saw another plunge in her health as a hacking cough and cold sent her into Maidstone Hospital for more antibiotics. This was bad news but our greater concern was that this infection wouldn't jeopardise her second chance of getting the Hickman line removed, scheduled for the following week. Georgie dreamt of a lovely deep bath in which she could lie down for the first time in seven months. After many sleepless nights, the cough and cold began to shift and to our joy the operation to remove the Hickman line went ahead. It wasn't just pulled out as we were expecting, but another incision was made halfway up her chest to release the little cuff which prevents the line from moving around. Georgie was very sore afterwards but jubilant that in just five days when the wound healed she would be able to have the Biggest Bubble Bath Ever and soak to her heart's content!

Thwarted again. The wound became infected and the

district nurse had to come and dress it and take a swab. Each evening she ran a high temperature, and to make matters worse the nasal gastric feeding pump kept getting blocked, setting off the alarm in the night. All the suggested remedies for unblocking the tube like lemonade, lemon juice, bicarb and warm water failed to sort it out, and we ended up having to go to Maidstone Hospital to have the tube pulled out and a new one passed, a horrible experience for Georgie. The next day we had to drive up to Great Ormond Street Hospital for an ultrasound scan because her persistent temperature and tummy pains were causing such concern at Maidstone, where they suggested it might possibly be appendicitis. The tests indicated it was probably a virus, and indeed Georgie began to improve a little and within a day or so she was able to have The Bath.

It was wonderful to watch her stretch out and completely submerge under water, bubbles and water going everywhere as she swished up and down the bath. What pleasure simple things can give when they have been denied. Very soon we progressed to the swimming pool and I was as exultant as Georgie to have some physical exercise after so many months of inactivity. Other steps forward included a weekly visit by a home tutor and we hoped that after half-term she would be able to go back to school for an afternoon after almost a year away.

She was never forgotten by her friends, though. They often phoned or visited if she was well enough and when we went to the school fete a tiny little girl spotted us at one of the stalls and ran, shouting excitedly to her mother, 'Mummy, Mummy, Georgie Sheldon's here!'

It was very touching to see how much they all cared

about her. One friend's mother, knowing Georgie's love of ballet, secretly and thoughtfully arranged a visit to the Royal Opera House, Covent Garden, to watch an afternoon dress rehearsal, starring Darcey Bussell. Georgie, her friend Zoe, her mum and I were royally treated, being chauffeur-driven to London and then seated in a box at the theatre for the performance. The visit backstage afterwards to meet her idol Darcey was wonderful. To be that close, to touch the costume, to smell the grease paint . . . I think I enjoyed it as much as the girls! They both fell happily asleep in the limousine on the way home and I felt so grateful for this kind outing that would give us lots to talk about in the difficult days ahead.

Another great encouragement was the finding of a night nurse who could come and sit with Georgie and allow me to get a proper night's sleep occasionally. Anne was a lovely lady who had forty years' nursing experience and had done night sitting for fifteen. She came for a trial run at ten o'clock and left at six, enabling me to feel I could sleep safely for the first time since September. It wasn't very easy for Georgie, having a stranger to care for her at night when she would much prefer her mum, but she was determined to give it a go, despite the fear she often faced in the darkness when the bad dreams assailed her. It was agreed that Anne would come twice a week, giving me a small chance to recharge my batteries.

With so much attention focused on Georgie it was inevitably very difficult for Mimi who was now fourteen and needing all the understanding and time any teenager does. She and I went up to London for a whole day's shopping together which was good for us both and I longed for more time to appreciate the intelligent, sensitive and attractive young woman who was emerging. Her faith was remarkable but she hated any sort of hypocrisy or insincerity with all the passionate idealism of youth. The slightest sign of being patronised or humoured and she would smoulder silently. But she also longed for normality more than anything. While others her age might dream of becoming film stars or going on exotic holidays, I think Mimi would have settled for stable, boring family life. Just to spend an evening at a friend's house made her feel guilty sometimes that she was enjoying herself when Georgie wasn't and it made all her friendships and social life so complicated. Should she tell Georgie of the exciting things she sometimes got up to, or was it better to hide them? Most of all I missed her spontaneity. It should have been a time of opportunity and excitement, but almost every decision was clouded by analysis and doubt.

It was June before we could say that we had had two 'good' days on the trot and then, briefly, we glimpsed the 'old' or rather the 'young' Georgie, which made us realise how much this illness had masked her true personality. That, indeed, was an underlying, unspoken grief, that we had subtly lost the little girl we knew.

Buoyed up by the signs of progress, Tom was busy polishing his hiking boots in preparation for the Three Peaks Challenge to raise money principally for the children's ambulance fund and two other charities. Heroically (as he told us) his team battled through snowfields and knife-edge ridges and despite getting lost and climbing four peaks instead of three (what can you expect from a bunch of surveyors?!) they completed the climbs and raised £16,500 for the charities.

And just as he scaled peaks and plunged into valleys, Georgie was again in the shadow of the mountain when he returned. Tonsillitis is not usually serious in itself but after cancer treatment it can knock a person for six. She was also deeply upset by the news that two little girl friends she had made in Great Ormond Street Hospital had died of their brain tumours, and Marcus – a special friend whose operation had been on the same day as Georgie's – had suddenly deteriorated having gone back to school, and now couldn't speak or walk, being paralysed all down his left side. It is so hard to maintain hope and confidence in the face of these cruel realities.

The same week I was invited to speak at Tonbridge Parish Church as part of their evangelism course; the first time I had given a talk since the previous summer, and I felt completely inadequate. Ironically I was also about to have a book published called, *The Blessing of Tears*, about weeping, although I had almost finished it by the time Georgie's cancer was discovered. Now I knew so much more about brokenness and it was out of my utter weakness that I tried to testify to God's love and goodness.

Perseverance was the key quality we sought to learn. And Mimi was clearly displaying it at school for at the end of term she was awarded not only the RE cup but also the Perseverance Cup for those with difficulties at home who had worked exceptionally hard throughout! If only one could move onto the next course once the proficiency certificate had been won. No, it seemed that there were ever higher grades and more difficult tests to be passed to perfect this grace.

The tonsillitis went and we had another long talk with

the consultant oncologist and the neurologist which resulted in their changing Georgie's medication to try and help the headaches and general nerve pains which plagued her so much. She appeared to pick up fleetingly but to our disbelief a rash suddenly appeared on her arm at the village fete and by the next day it had spread all across her chest causing her much pain and discomfort. Shingles. No swimming and no school visits for a week and a hard, lonely week doing jigsaws and watching TV. By the following week, however, she was feeling a little brighter and even came to the village hall barn dance where she joined in a few dances, but had to stand on the sidelines while Mimi entertained her friends with an energetic charity tennis tournament in aid of the children's ambulance.

High summer was with us, the long holiday stretched ahead, and it seemed at last as if we had come into calmer water. By popular demand, we again went on a Christian house-party in Shropshire for a week and enjoyed the excellent teaching of Bishop Peter Lee, coming home physically fitter (if a little exhausted) and spiritually refreshed after a packed schedule. The best news was that Georgie was pretty much able to keep up with the other youngsters. She played badminton, swam, did some trampolining and appeared in the final cabaret, seeming to get stronger and more confident as the week progressed. Mimi too had a wonderful time, quite free from anxieties and restrictions, and both girls pronounced it the best 'God Week' they had ever been on!

On our return, Georgie's gastric nasal tube was removed on a trial basis to see if she could maintain her weight without the overnight feeding. It was wonderful for her to be free of all bits of plastic sticking out of her! Another lengthy MRI scan was followed by a glorious week in Cheshire on a narrow-boat which gave us an excellent opportunity for enforced relaxation and all of us came back feeling strengthened and rested, more able to cope with whatever news we might have to face at Great Ormond Street Hospital.

In trepidation we waited to see the surgeon who performed Georgie's operation nearly a year ago. Only a year? It seemed like five. My mind raced with all the possibilities he might present us with, and it was difficult to keep up the bright chatter with Georgie. Suddenly our name was called and my heart missed a beat. But the surgeon's smiling face said it all. He was delighted to announce that there were no signs at all of recurrence of the tumour in her head or spine and she wouldn't need another scan for six months. Children often do well after surgery, he explained, only to be really knocked down by the chemo and radiotherapy . . . The symptoms which persisted, we began to dare to believe, were due to the treatment rather than the cancer and we allowed ourselves to celebrate the prospect of health, recovery and normality. Our phone positively hummed with people sharing our good news and joy, and we really thanked God for the renewed hope we had been given.

On 2 September Georgie celebrated her eleventh birthday – with great enthusiasm and relief, it has to be said, for, as she confided in me, she 'hadn't really enjoyed being ten'. We remembered poignantly her birthday the year before when she had inexplicably been feeling so ill and we really thanked God that he had brought us safely this far.

The next hurdle was school. Georgie could hardly believe that she had ever had the energy to do a whole day as just an hour to start with was exhausting, but we prayed that her energy levels and stamina would pick up. Unfortunately the first two lessons of her first day back were double maths and I'm sure that would have given most of us the headache she came out with. These persistent headaches were actually continuing to be of great concern. She had to take pain-killers every day just to keep them under control and they created a scenario where Georgie appeared all right but really was not. Her hair was beginning to grow back, but in some ways this was more difficult than being bald as with the short, downy tufts she kept being mistaken for a boy:

'Let the young man through the door.'

'Would he like a drink?'

'What's your son's name?'

This greatly damaged her self-esteem and she needed lots of reassurance that she was still pretty and feminine. We fixed an appointment at the beauty salon to have her ears pierced in the hope that this might improve her female identity – but by today's fashion even that wasn't guaranteed!

Exactly a year since the tumour was diagnosed! We were so thankful that we still had our lovely daughter, that she had come through the surgery, chemo and radio-therapy, was able to walk and talk and even try a bit of school. Conscious of so many blessings it would have been easy to overlook the daily inner battles Georgie still had to fight. From her point of view she described herself as very, very tired 90 per cent of the time and with a headache for the other 10 per cent. Stamina and joy continued to be our chief prayers. We had gained the height of this ridge at great cost. Sometimes we felt we had reached the summit only to find that a cloud had protected us from realising that the final peak was still a long way off. As the view cleared over the next few days we realised with growing shock that our ascent had barely begun. We hadn't yet endured to the end.

9

A woman . . . cried unto him, saying, Have mercy on me, O Lord, thou son of David . . . But he answered her not a word.

Matthew 15:22–3, AV

The path began to descend and it became increasingly difficult to see how we could keep a firm footing. It was a bewildering slide and that was the hardest part of the next few months – trying to come to terms with such a disintegration of the hopes which had begun to grow. After cancer, every physical disorder is cloaked in threat. A cough cannot be a symptom of just a simple cold, and indeed no cold is simple when the immune system is so depressed. An irritating sore throat became a chest infection which in turn degenerated into pleurisy. Georgie had such a rattle in her chest that you could hear it in the next room and, with a lot of pain in her back and shoulders too, she generally felt very unwell. Her return to school was shelved, therefore, and even the home tutor was cancelled. Antibiotics seemed to overcome the infection temporarily but increased headaches and sickness were the price and within days her condition had deteriorated so much that she was in and out of hospital, both the Middlesex and Great Ormond Street. A CT scan showed nothing sinister and the consultant tried to reassure us that it was simply the pleurisy which had pulled her right down. We just prayed that she would begin to gain strength again.

Another canal boat holiday was booked for the October half-term and we were in two minds as to whether there was any point in trying to take it but we remembered the happy time we had spent there in the summer and hoped we could reproduce it. Bad move. Despite beautiful weather on the North Oxford and Grand Union Canals in a fully heated comfortable narrow-boat, Georgie was just too ill to be able to enjoy it at all and we gave up and came home.

This was worse than anything that had gone before. She seemed to have completely run out of steam and was unable to walk any distance at all. Getting up in the morning took all her energy and she had to go back to bed to sleep, needing two or three more sleeps during the day just to keep going. She had to be carried up and downstairs, helped with dressing, and the smallest things, even conversation, tired her out. As the day wore on she sometimes felt a little better, only to start the whole miserable process off again the next morning.

Dr Charles, the consultant who first saw Georgie at Maidstone Hospital, came to visit her at home and it was clear that she would need a battery of tests as soon as possible to discover what was at the root of this relapse. Georgie was admitted to the endocrinology department of the Middlesex Hospital and there she underwent three days of extensive tests on the thyroid, adrenal and pituitary glands, and an insulin tolerance test. Within a few days the results came through. The consultant explained Georgie's pituitary gland had been affected, probably by the radiotherapy, and Georgie was producing only enough cortisol to get by. As cortisol is responsible for giving you the 'get up and go' in life, it became clear that Georgie was only making enough to 'get up' and insufficient 'to go'. On top of this she was not producing any growth hormone at all and was therefore 'metabolically insufficient'. She was immediately placed on steroids and began nightly injections of growth hormone which she would have to continue until she was at least sixteen. Still more tests followed as the hospital endeavoured to get the balance of medication just right and to see an improvement in the terrible fatigue, sickness, headaches and weakness.

By now another Christmas was approaching, and it seemed incredible that we were struggling almost more with the effects of cancer than we had been a year before. We sometimes feared that our friends must tire of praying for us constantly, and felt we ought to be able to 'reward' them with good news. It was hard to keep on updating the message line with perplexing accounts of fresh setbacks and struggles. So often we expressed our thanks in the message, but were particularly struck by one reply which said, 'We don't need thanks for our prayers for Georgie; it's a privilege to pray for her.'

So on we prayed; prayed for small things: for stamina and more energy; for the headaches to decrease; for less sickness and pain; for greater strength and for growth. The hospital provided physio and hydrotherapy to try and build up her wasted limbs, and she was able to attend the hospital Christmas party, having her photograph taken with some handsome footballer and the stars of *Birds of a Feather*. Before she could come home she had to get used to injecting herself in the thigh or the stomach with the nightly hormones, a dreaded procedure for an eleven-year-old girl who hated needles. She enjoyed perfecting her technique on any willing adult and we were very touched when Colin, the children's ambulance driver for that day, volunteered his own thigh – a real needle, but no growth hormone for this ex fire chief! She was incredibly brave, and although a little shaky was determined to master the skill and spend Christmas at home.

We were almost too exhausted to notice Christmas, let alone celebrate it. By the end of the day I was feeling rotten and promptly went down with flu followed by Mimi and Georgie. Tom was left to don his nurse's pinny and do the Florence Nightingale bit. It wasn't easy to bounce back. We all felt sapped of energy for many days and Georgie crashed down again with a high temperature and a cough.

We were losing our little girl. Not so much physically, though it sometimes seemed that her frail body just wouldn't be able to fight any more, but spiritually, emotionally. Her light was dimming. Her sparkling smile was seldom seen. Her vivacity and energy seemed like an almost forgotten dream. She began to lose her hope and her courage.

'I don't think I'll ever feel better, Mum,' she whispered one night. And I had to summon every ounce of faith and strength to will her to keep going, to encourage her not to give up to but to keep on persevering.

That sort of effort takes its toll. I so much wanted to take her pain and her bewilderment. To suffer it all myself and let her go free. The feelings of anger and injustice, which I hadn't had a problem with before, began to gnaw at my peace.

Questions.

No answers.

Fear.

Not just fear of the future. But fear of losing heart, losing hope, losing faith, losing him who had been my love and my strength. My Jesus. No longer mine.

Georgie felt she had been left behind, that she was now just an onlooker as her friends talked about entrance exams and eleven-plus. Their other topics of conversation, about parties, fashions and pop stars, sometimes seemed pointless and irrelevant to her, especially as insecurities about her own attractiveness began to surface. It was a constant endeavour to keep her animated and enthused, especially as the effort was so exhausting for her. She described the pain in her head as like having her head impaled on a spike, and concentration and activity were equally impossible for her. Jack, her beautiful white cat, now full grown, became one of her few sources of pleasure. He was extraordinarily empathetic for a cat and was content to lie in her arms for hours, purring and luxuriating in her constant caresses. I'm sure he talked to her! She certainly confided in him many things which I suspect she could barely admit to herself.

The dark days of winter passed into a dreary spring and still Georgie was racked with pain and weakness. Tests and scans continued until eventually a neurologist put a name to the problem. Tonsillitis, shingles and pleurisy all in a row last September; three viral illnesses hitting a severely depressed immune defence system: Georgie had ME.

It wasn't so much a diagnosis as just another mountain to climb. Everyone knows that ME isn't something you can take a pill for and be cured. In fact I realised that this really described her *condition* – chronic fatigue – rather than identifying a particular root which could be addressed. Nobody could say exactly what had caused this ultimate deterioration but it was probably a combination of the after-effects of surgery, chemo, radiotherapy and the infections. How could we break the spiral of metabolic breakdown and physical weakness? The doctors seemed as perplexed as we were.

It didn't seem possible that Georgie could get any weaker, but she did. A meeting of fifteen people associated with Georgie's treatment and care was called to try and agree the best way forward. In the short term they decided that she should be readmitted to the Middlesex Hospital for extensive tests, an EEG and a review of her pain control, before moving to Great Ormond Street Hospital to be assessed fully by the neurologist. The results showed, depressingly, that her adrenal function was even less than in November but the doctors were at a loss to be able to explain this. Their focus became how to get Georgie back into school and normal life, so attention

now switched to devising a detailed rehabilitation programme.

The concept of rehabilitation has its supporters and its
critics. A rigorous and gruelling regime, it involves not
asking the patient how they are feeling as this might put
the focus back on the illness. Instead the emphasis is on
goals and possibilities, on providing a structured frame-
work of medical support, including treatment and physio,
with reintegration into normal life through a gradually
increasing timetable of activities.

For Georgie this was the biggest battle yet. After several
weeks in hospital she was sent home to continue her
struggle to regain strength. She went to school for half an
hour each day, despite being barely able to walk and often
being very sick, but she refused to give up. It was heartbreaking to see her putting her weary body and soul into
the programme and yet to be unable really to comfort and
support her for fear of undermining her psychologically.
Looking back we are appalled that we put her through
this, but at the time we were so desperate we would have
tried almost anything.

And then she got shingles. Again. As if that wasn't
enough of a blow, I then got them too. Where was God's
help and kindness in all this? It was utterly bewildering.
All our family and friends rallied for another mighty
onslaught of prayer, my brother Nigel coming over from
America to spend a lot of time praying with Georgie. We
were as angry as we were upset with the situation. Yet still
the consultants kept on adding a little bit more to the
rehabilitation programme each time we saw them. As
soon as Georgie recovered from the shingles, her school
commitment was increased to two lessons a day. And

straight away we saw a significant worsening of her tiredness. She began to get muddled and confused and her nights were haunted by awful nightmares so that she never really rested and regained energy. Someone misheard me discussing the new regime and thought it was a 'debilitating programme' rather than a rehabilitation programme! That was the last thing we wanted but it was perilously near the truth as we watched Georgie floundering, at times weeping brokenly and saying she just couldn't go on.

Somehow we struggled on to the end of term. Georgie had been at this school since the age of three so it was a big day when she said goodbye to all her teachers and many of her friends. Significantly she was awarded a special cup for perseverance but no trophy could adequately symbolise the desperate battle she was going through to hang on to her faith and her courage. Delighted though we were at this recognition, we knew all too well that the war was not yet won, and that only those who 'endured to the end' would receive 'the crown of life'.

The start of the summer holidays meant a change in the very strict rehab programme and with the warmer weather we hoped to be able to do some swimming and so increase Georgie's physical strength a little. Walking even small distances was still utterly exhausting for her. And if only we could rekindle a little of her joy. Once again we soared up on the seesaw of hopes and longings. Surely now we would see some progress.

I dreaded having to change the message on the prayer line and often deliberately left it for days, weeks, because I couldn't bear to report the apparent absence of any answer to our prayers. In a sense, having no structure and immediate goals made it even harder and it was so draining for me, trying to keep Georgie going. The terrible headaches and nightmares continued and inexorably her spirits sank lower and lower. Another week's house-party in Somerset did something to encourage our faltering steps and we even managed to go to Normandy for four days with Tom's family, twenty-five of us in one household! Not the most restful of breaks but an effective distraction for Georgie and she managed to walk a little further and enjoy some of the beautiful surroundings. When we got back home, the lovely garden she had planted in the spring was ablaze with colour, and her sunflowers were about ten feet tall. Sadly one had been crushed and broken in a storm, and I was transfixed by its bent and splintered stem. As long as I had breath, I would fight to prevent Georgie becoming that flower.

On returning from holiday, we noticed that Georgie began having blank spells when she would stare into space, motionless, or not respond when we spoke to her. The consultant at Great Ormond Street Hospital felt that it might be some sort of partial seizure and so changed her drugs in case they might be the cause. We had just come to terms with that when, on the evening of her birthday, she became very unwell with a racing pulse which left her breathless and exhausted. This galloping heart rate continued even when she was asleep so she was swept straight back into Great Ormond Street Hospital for yet more tests. Initially it was thought that it must be the new drugs but there was always the possibility that it might be her adrenal glands malfunctioning again. In the end it took several weeks to ascertain that it was a toxic reaction to one of the drugs but in the meantime she was reduced to a state of utter collapse and back in a wheelchair as her body reacted as though it was permanently running a marathon.

September was upon us and Georgie was distraught that she wasn't able to start her senior school. She really wanted to avoid falling further and further behind and longed to cease being a mere spectator on life. With her continuing weakness, however, we had to accept that something radical had to happen if she was to be able to attend at all in the near future. And so began the agonising deliberation over a 'last resort' idea which was to prove such a costly and damaging decision that we were to feel we had betrayed our daughter.

10

How long wilt thou forget me, O Lord? for ever? how long wilt thou hide thy face from me?

Psalm 13:1, AV

In Great Ormond Street Hospital, behind a locked door, there was a ward called the Mildred Creek Unit. It housed ten patients, five of whom had serious eating disorders such as anorexia and bulimia, and it aimed to adjust behaviour and improve physical and mental health by a rigorous regime of duties, responsibilities, study and exercise. The doctors felt strongly that Georgie should be admitted to the unit for two or three months, living there from Monday to Friday and just coming home for weekends. Without distractions, in a positive and structured environment, they were sure her body would begin to readjust to greater demands and success would be self-perpetuating.

It seemed logical and sensible but we were filled with terrible misgivings. The unit had an unwelcoming feel and its locked doors and bars on the windows made it seem like a prison. The staff appeared caring enough but were their smiles just a little shallow and brittle? Why did the dark gaze of the emaciated girls follow us with such a look of pain and longing? The unit was tiny for so many children, really no more than a small apartment, and it included a school room and kitchen as well as dormitories. Georgie would be expected to do three hours of lessons every morning and then a variety of therapies or exercises in the afternoon which might involve a mile walk to the swimming pool. Families were discouraged from visiting too often, twice a week was recommended and really only a parent was allowed. Our hearts sank as we looked round it, but we were at the end of all our own ideas and thus reliant on the medical advice of those who had cared for Georgie so well for over two years. Desperately we sought advice from everyone we could think of, but nobody could come up with any viable alternative for Georgie's severe ME, and in the end, after writing a list of the pros and cons, and talking at length with Georgie herself, we felt we should give it a try.

Looking back I wondered at first why I didn't stick to my instincts but I know that at the time we felt so anxious and helpless that we might have agreed to almost anything the doctors suggested. This extreme mental vulnerability is a factor not duly considered, I suspect, by doctors who may feel that they have laid the situation clearly before parents and invited them to feel included in the decision. For us, the final decision felt like no choice at all. The doctors had pronounced. It was the Best Thing. We must accept it.

Bursting with life: Georgie in August 1995

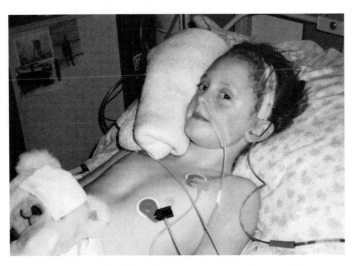

Fighting for life: Georgie in September 1995

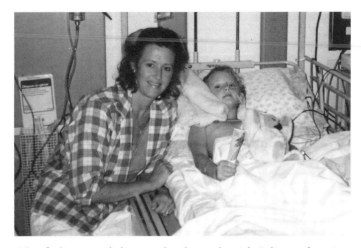

'I'm feeling much better, thank you!': with Julie, and an ice lolly, six hours after the operation

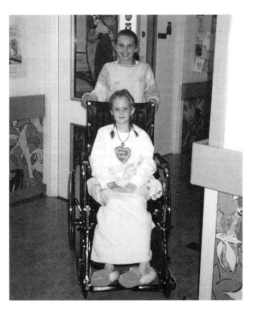

Special friends: Georgie and Annabel

Playing 'Doctors and Nurses': Georgie with Mimi (left)
and "Dr Georgie"

Cold heads need hats!: the baseball cap collection

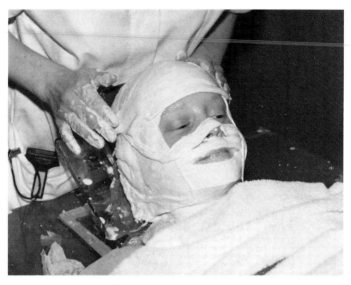

Moulding the radiotherapy mask

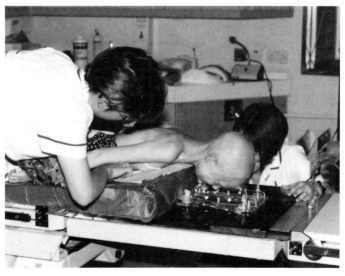

Georgie is bolted head down for radiotherapy

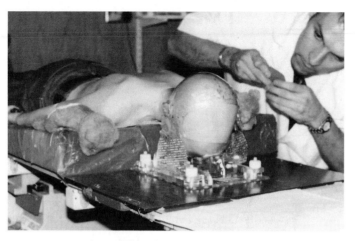

The teddies also got the treatment

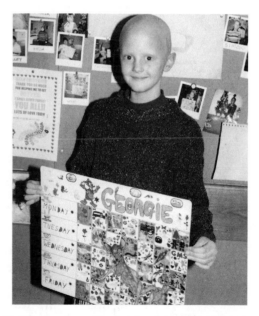

Finished at last: Georgie's sticker chart for the
33 completed treatments

Georgie and Ross surrounded by school friends and Peggy Wood in the Children's Ambulance

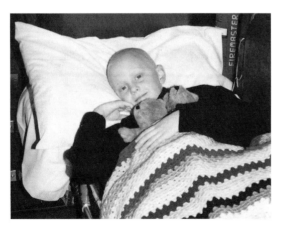

Travelling in comfort in the Children's Ambulance

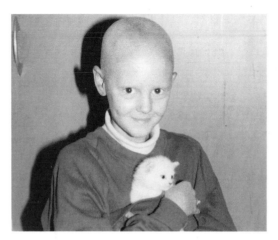

Georgie and her "angel", Jack

Dancing dream: Georgie and Zoe meet Darcey Bussell

Narrow boat, narrow horizon: Mimi, Julie and Georgie
at the time ME/Chronic Fatigue began

Secure at Burrswood with Thomas the cat

With dread. Taking Georgie in on the first day was like sending her into a remand home. It was so unlike the rest of the hospital where many improvements and building works had created a modern, first-rate children's hospital. She seemed to be allowed so few personal belongings and indeed there was very little space by her cramped sleeping area to store anything, and even what she had was carefully searched for any instruments with which patients could harm themselves. We were shocked but felt we had to go along with the rules. And Rules, we came to realise, ruled.

Great store was set on collective responsibility and punishment. The day started with a team of two or three patients – none of them older than fifteen, one as young as ten – making breakfast for all the other children. This involved asking everyone what they would like but certain items were compulsory because so many of the patients had eating disorders. Breakfast would drag on for as long as an hour and lunch for much longer because every single scrap of food on the plate had to be finished. The anorexics would push their food around their plate or try to smuggle it into their clothes, and any failure to eat or discovery of subterfuge resulted in everyone having to sit in silence for another half an hour or be denied their trip to the park. The schoolroom was actually a more positive environment than the residential side, and Georgie found a crumb of solace there despite the physical exhaustion of having to sit for three hours when she could barely concentrate for three minutes. As for walking to the swimming pool or park, Georgie was not allowed to use the wheelchair but had to haul herself along the streets, many times on the point of collapse, and continually trailing along behind the others.

The reality of life inside the unit only came to light bit by bit. The three hours spent in the schoolroom were the most positive part of the day; the remaining twenty-one hours can be described only as miserable. Georgie was ill with flu in her first week so we thought that might account for the very negative account she gave when she first came home for the weekend. She cried desperately when I took her back, but surely it was inevitable that she would be homesick for a while. She said the nurses were sharp and unkind, but were they merely trying to jolly the inmates along and ensure an orderly and positive environment? We didn't know what to think, but we had to trust that the doctors knew best. The strain on all of us intensified and first came to a head when Georgie had been in the unit for about ten days.

Mimi was only allowed to visit her sister twice a week and even this seemed to be frowned upon. To bypass the unsatisfactory situation of yet another stilted conversation in her cramped dormitory, we asked, one evening, if we could all go out for a meal with Georgie as a family. Permission was granted and we set off for a nearby hotel to have, we hoped, a more relaxed and happy time. But before we had even ordered we realised that Georgie was in a terrible state. It wasn't that she cried, that would have been easier, but she just kept saying in a quiet, flat voice, 'I want to die. It's hell in there.'

Fear and anxiety rose in us all. Desperate to try and push her mind into a more positive frame, I pleaded with her to keep on going, to persevere with the treatment, but voices became raised. Then suddenly I realised that Mimi was white and shaking.

'I can't bear it,' she cried. 'I just can't bear any more of this!'

It was more than just emotion. She stumbled to her feet and nearly fell. We helped her to the ladies cloakroom where she collapsed, sick and dizzy, gasping for breath and complaining of ringing in her ears. I knew the signs. This was not illness but panic. The human mind and frame can take only so much tension and anxiety, and young Mimi, at only fifteen, had had to carry too much. But how could she be comforted and who could comfort her? Georgie found it very difficult that her sister said she couldn't cope when it was Georgie who actually had to undergo the horrors of separation from her family and a clinical regime. In the immediate term we had to get Georgie back to the MCU and persuade her to stick at it a little longer, though we had just heard that the doctors felt the treatment should be extended to four months. When we got back to the unit, Mimi had another panic attack and had to be helped out by Tom. It was the last time she went to see her sister there.

For Mimi this was the start of a great deal of mental anguish. So much bitterness and anger raged inside her. Worries big and small robbed her of all her peace. She was in the thick of her GCSEs and desperately worried about her work when so much time and emotional space was taken up with Georgie's illness. She resented the fact that her school had not taken the pressure off academic studies by allowing her to miss some homework, for example, if she had to go to the hospital, but it was a highly competitive school and achievement was the chief goal. No one had offered her support, reasoning, I expect, that because she kept her feelings to herself she was coping fine, the usual scenario. But now she was in deep need.

Fear began to dominate her: fear of further panic attacks which made her terrified of confined spaces, of the school bus, of public places like the cinema, of staying at people's houses. She was also scared that all her anger would burst out in a string of abuse at those she felt had not understood her pain. About three times a week she was gripped with an overwhelming sense of anxiety and terror until eventually the school did recognise her suffering and arranged counselling for her which helped her a great deal.

Much of this I only realised some time later, for Mimi found it hard to share her grief and fear with the family when we, she felt, were so caught up with Georgie's difficulties. Strain and hurt was written right across all the relationships in the family, even though we needed each other so much and loved each other so much – or perhaps because of that. Our emotional resources to meet the needs of those closest to us had run out.

Back in the unit, things were getting worse for Georgie. Because almost every moment of the day was organised and supervised, it was very difficult for her to find a moment of privacy and quiet for 'talking to Jesus', as she put it. The only haven of refuge in her day was the half-hour they were allowed on their beds after lunch and then she used to switch on her worship tapes on her Walkman and try to lift up her spirit to Jesus. She also had a diary, written in secret under her bedcovers, which was a kind of friend and confidante. It makes harrowing reading now – a heartbreaking record. In the end nothing could hide what was really going on there. She complained that the nurses were physically cruel to her, slapping and pushing her, and one weekend I found marks on her body, perhaps of self-harm, perhaps inflicted by someone else, we'll never know. We had to get her out of that nightmare immediately. It has been little consolation that the terrible treatment of those poor children was eventually uncovered and became the subject of a recent BBC *Panorama* documentary. Nobody had to tell us that appalling harm had been done to a very vulnerable and sick child. We were devastated.

It is impossible to convey the mental pain which now enwrapped us all. Anger, self-reproach, bitterness, anxiety and fear gripped us in a black embrace which threatened to suck us down and drown us in despair. Where could we turn now? Who could provide help for a child not only physically ill but in a state of severe depression? How could we talk about what had happened without fear of reprisals by the medical profession which might jeopardise Georgie's future treatment? And who would believe us anyway? I think we would not have survived if we hadn't found two charities.

The first was the Ellenor Foundation. I had telephoned all the major cancer charities, hoping to find one that might to be able to offer support at home, but it appeared that paediatric cover was hard to come by in our area. If it was an adult needing care, we could have received any number of home support nurses, but there was definitely a gap for children at home. A 'chance' conversation with a friend put us in touch with the Ellenor Foundation, which offered specialist help at home to patients of all ages. This in reality meant that there was at last a twenty-four-hour link with a specialist nurse, respite care at home which enabled me to pop out and do the food shopping, and general support at home for the whole family.

Second, and as Georgie was initially too traumatised and unwell to come straight home, there was Burrswood. Burrswood is a Christian centre for healthcare and ministry where people come to find healing through skilled nursing, medical expertise, counselling and prayer. Set in the beautiful surroundings of the Kent/Sussex borders, the lovely nineteenth-century house and its tranquil grounds offer a peaceful environment ideal for healing and regeneration. Unlike an ordinary hospital, it treats the whole person – body, mind and spirit. Its uniqueness lies in its blend of medicine, prayer and individual counselling, aiming to keep the love of Christ at the heart of care and to be a sign of the kingdom of God in a hurting world.

Why hadn't we turned there first of all? When cancer has ravaged your family, you can become very dependent on the medical experts, the specialist doctors and hospitals who are at the forefront of scientific knowledge in the fight against terminal illness. Shocked, frightened and uninformed, you feel you have no choice but to trust the great names whose expertise is legendary. The terrifying momentum of the disease and its conventional treatment sweeps you along and you feel powerless to alter the direction or slow the pace. Alternatives are not really laid before you, or at least none which are not conveyed as risky or foolish. You feel trapped and impotent. That is not to say that much of Georgie's care wasn't sensitively and effectively handled by kind and gifted medical personnel.

But in the end the system was not able to cope with the

extreme emotional, psychological and spiritual needs not only of Georgie but of the whole family. The past three years had not simply been Georgie's battle; we had all been in it together, and now individually and collectively we were broken and desperately in need of healing. Burrswood saw that totality and was able to offer the beginning of the rebuilding process. It was to prove far more difficult than we could have anticipated, however. When limbs are broken, we can put on bandages, casts, splints and even new parts; when hearts and spirits are crushed, the healing process is much more complex. And Georgie and I, in particular, had now come to the end of all joy and strength. The only thing left was our faith. We thought we had reached the bottom of the pit. I didn't anticipate that it was possible to lose even faith and be in a place of utter hopelessness and despair. I hadn't imagined that there might come a time when I simply would not be able to cope anymore, when my ability to endure the pain and persevere with the struggle would come to an end. My heart and spirit were damaged beyond repair. God foresaw that patching them up would be no long-term solution. A transplant was what he had in mind. His anaesthetic was to be my 'dark night of the soul'.

11

I sought him, but I found him not.
Song of Songs 3:1, AV

'Mum, in the last three years my life has seemed like a jigsaw which has been taken apart and the pieces scattered all over the floor. But now it's as if Jesus has the lid with the picture and is beginning to put it all together again.'

After three weeks in Burrswood, Georgie's eyes had already begun to sparkle just a little on occasions. Withdrawn, blank and exhausted, she had barely noticed her new beautiful surroundings when she arrived, but day by day she responded to the atmosphere of loving care and acceptance, so different from the hostile and harsh regime of the MCU. It wasn't easy for her to start trusting adults again, so traumatised was she by the rejection and cruelty she had just suffered. But the patience and understanding of all the staff at Burrswood gradually coaxed her from the cave of her isolation and pain. It could only be one small step at a time, though. Her headaches, joint pains, sickness and fatigue still plagued her just as much, and the lack of appreciable improvement in these areas tempered the encouragement of her emotional progress.

Each day relaxing hydrotherapy and rest was interspersed with counselling and help from a team of sensitive and inspired staff. The physician, Dr Paul Worthley, assessed her medical needs with extraordinary care and wisdom, spending hours sitting on her bed, listening to her, drawing her out, even spending time teaching her the guitar, letting her know that he understood her pain and could help her. The assessment of her physical needs was made in close collaboration with Lynne, one of the counsellors at the centre, and Steve from the chaplaincy team. Not only was Georgie's suffering embraced and borne by these people, but my own distress was equally considered. Indeed, the whole family were brought together on several occasions to enable us to understand, share and support the pain of the others.

I wish I could say that at last our troubles were over and that now, steadily, we climbed out of the pit. As with bereavement, there is often a delayed reaction in cases of extreme trauma, and the deepest grief does not surface until much later, often when the initial support has been withdrawn. Fortunately for me the human support was there when God began his open-heart surgery on me but my agony was that I began to lose my confidence that *he* was there. He had been my rock, my refuge, my fortress and my friend for so many years. Now I was in darkness, calling for him but unable to find his hand.

One of the hardest things was not being able to talk about what was happening inside me, not even with Tom, really. It didn't seem legitimate, allowable, that I might be drastically in need of help myself. There is no time for introspection and navel-gazing when you're a carer. Or so I thought. There seemed to be demands on my attention and energy from all sides and from everyone. I stayed in Burrswood with Georgie which was wonderful, but yet again I was abandoning Mimi who had her mock GCSEs coming up and depending on my parents and friends to look after my home. Christmas was only days away and, as for any mother, there was a host of things to do in preparation and no time.

But at least, again, we were together for Christmas. We went through all the usual festive rituals, smiled and laughed in all the right places but inside me something seemed to have died. 'God so loved the world that he sent his only son . . .' Baby Jesus, sent out of love for me? Died to save me? After years of solid faith and acceptance, suddenly now even the most basic tenets of the creed just didn't make sense for me. Just hang on in there, I thought. Burn-out, exhaustion, that's all. Everybody has times of doubt. All things pass.

But this didn't. Over the coming weeks, as Georgie returned to Burrswood and continued to make very slow but steady progress, I remained in darkness. I wept frequently and brokenly, but there was little sense of comfort. Repeatedly I picked myself up, dusted myself down and said, 'Pull yourself together.' Pat, the Head of Counselling at Burrswood, noticed my need and we arranged to meet up and begin talking about some of this. I soon became very grateful for, not only her wisdom, but the way she was quietly beside me – not giving clever advice, but guiding me through the darkness by offering a place to 'tell it as it really was'. During the time I spent with Pat, Georgie would play endless games of Scrabble with a friend she had made: Jonathan. The age difference of about seventy years made this a special relationship, and they would laugh and joke together as they invented more and more outrageous words.

Encouragingly, a visit with Georgie to the neurologist and endocrinologist revealed that she had grown nearly four inches in the past year, and her MRI scan showed no recurrence of the cancer anywhere. Her physical strength was gradually increasing and by March Georgie was managing to go into school for an hour or so twice a week.

The aspect which didn't improve and continued to be a great strain was her recurrent nightmares. Terrifying dreams haunted her every night and meant little sleep for us both. While Georgie was able to rest during the day, it was almost impossible for me, and although we were joined by all those praying in a day of fasting, the nightmares still stalked her. It was suggested that these might be the result of the drugs she still had to take and it was a relief when the endocrinolgist suggested quite independently that she should be taken off the steroids. Sadly it made no difference to the dreams. On the day of the fast, though, a couple of us sat on the bed with her at Burrswood and could sense a real letting go of some of the past hurts and distress from the hospital stays and traumas.

And there were significant steps forward elsewhere. Georgie took up piano lessons again and it was particularly poignant to hear her playing when the last time she had tried three years before was the first clear indication of her tumour. She won a makeover from a children's magazine and modelled tracksuit bottoms which did a lot for her self-confidence. And in a week of glorious early summer sunshine we couldn't resist another adorable white kitten with blue eyes, who was a half-sister to her beloved Jack. And then Jack himself became a celebrity! To our amazement, Jack won the Golden Arthur Award 1998 and Georgie was awarded a huge £1,200 cash prize and a year's supply of cat food! To enter for this 'prestigious' award, contestants had to write a letter explaining why their cat was special and how it had helped them. This was Georgie's contribution:

Dear Arthur the Cat

Hello. My name is Georgie and I have a white cat called Jack. He looks just like you. He is really cool, cuddly and very cute!

I have been very ill with Cancer and while I was ill I saw an Arthur's cat advert on the television and from then on, I have really wanted a white cat. We phoned around everywhere but no one had a white cat with kittens. Then one day a cat called Puff had a litter of kittens. She had one white one. There in the middle of the box among four other kittens was a little white one with an actual golden halo on his head. I knew from then on that he was the one I had been looking for. He was given to me and six weeks later, after visiting him every spare minute I had, I brought him home and he has been the best and most devoted cat ever since.

He has just had his second birthday and I gave him some treats and toys and I really spoiled him. For a going home present Jack brought me a mouse which went missing and two nights later I found it in my room at four in the morning. (Well, it's the thought that counts, isn't it?)

He likes to bounce on the trampoline with me when it is warm but when I try to stroke him I electrify him because the trampoline is so static!

Jack is so affectionate and is always posing and wanting to have his picture taken. He has really helped me through some very difficult times and has always been there for me, just waiting for a hug!!

Jack is so adorable and a very special cat.

Georgie and Jack were awarded their prize at a glittering ceremony at BAFTA in Piccadilly, home of the British film industry. It was a fantastic experience for any child and they appeared on television and radio and in countless newspapers and magazines. With her prize money Georgie bought a candy floss machine and over the next few months she did a roaring trade at various fetes and functions, showing a canny eye for business. This success and excitement brought her great pleasure but also indicated the inner resilience and resourcefulness which had carried her through the terrors of the past few years. Mimi also emerged with an astounding clutch of seven grade A passes, one A* and one B at GCSE, demonstrating her own extraordinary courage and determination. Tom's new business venture was going from strength to strength and he was feeling confident and positive. Why was I being such a failure, then?

Out of the blue we received a telephone call from some relatives. 'How would you all like a holiday? We've bought two weeks in a charity auction and we'd like you to have it!'

This holiday was in a beautiful home in Jamaica, and as we looked at the photographs it seemed to be a dream come true. We were able to take two very special friends of the girls, Fenella and Annabel, and together we all felt incredibly excited, happy and blessed. I did indeed realise how very fortunate we were, and when Hurricane Mitch graciously decided to change course and avoid our particular Caribbean island I felt extremely grateful! The house and situation we stayed in were idyllic and Georgie made a superhuman effort to make the most of the opportunity. There was much laughter, card-playing and learning the proper way to reggae. We swam, we read, and Tom and I celebrated our nineteenth wedding anniversary in luxury and style.

On our return, however, Georgie experienced a considerable backlash from the flight and crashed very low. As ever it was me who had to pick up the pieces and provide the emotional impetus to pick her up and keep her going. This time, somehow, I just couldn't do it. It felt as if I had been giving a blood transfusion out of my own veins for years and now my whole lifeblood had run dry. In one split second, in a devastating moment of crystal perception, I suddenly knew that what I most greatly feared had come upon me. Jesus was no longer there. I was standing on the edge of a cliff and suddenly he had gone. He had stood beside me for twenty-three years and now he was nowhere to be seen. His constant support, friendship and love had been withdrawn. I was alone. I had lost my faith.

I've watched a labrador sitting at his master's feet. His eyes are on his master's face, watching for any command, sign of love or tasty titbit. But if that dog receives no signal or encouragement, he loses interest and becomes sleepy. He looks away. He looks down. If there was never another word or act of care from the master, ultimately he would probably die.

For almost a year it felt as if the Master had been looking away. For whatever reason, his face had been turned away as I sat waiting at his feet, watching and waiting for the familiar commands, the looks of love, the food to bless and strengthen. But there had been nothing. No direction, no peace, no love, and worst of all, no assurance of the Master's presence.

Would it be possible to persevere through this too? Would there ever *be* an end to this darkness? I didn't feel so much as if *I* had given up but as if God had given *me* up. Yet I was reminded of the saying, 'When God feels far away, guess who moved.' I began to search through the writings of people we have come to call saints to see if it was possible to go through such a crisis and yet to recover as strong a faith as before. In doing so I was heartened by the depths out of which St Therese of Lisieux cried hundreds of years before me:

I was in a sad desert, or rather my soul was like a fragile boat delivered up to the mercy of the waves and having no pilot. I knew Jesus was there sleeping in my boat, but the night was so black it was impossible to see Him; nothing gave me light, not a single flash came to break the dark clouds. No doubt lightning is a dismal sight but at least if the storm had broken out in earnest I would have been able to see Jesus for one passing moment. But it was night! The dark night of the soul! I felt I was all alone in the garden of Gethsemane like Jesus, and I found no consolation on earth or from heaven; God Himself seemed to have abandoned me.

(*Story of a Soul*, ICS Publications, Washington)

Somehow I had to find him again.

12

Drop thy still dews of quietness
  Till all our strivings cease;
Take from our souls the strain and stress
  And let our ordered lives confess
    The beauty of thy peace.

Breathe through the heats of our desire
  Thy coolness and thy balm;
  Let sense be dumb, let flesh retire,
Breathe through the earthquake, wind and fire,
  O still small voice of calm!

John Greenleaf Whittier

At the summer house-party a year before, a young woman when praying had had a picture, a thought, of someone with a long splinter in their hand, an old wound, which necessitated the top layer of skin being removed and the splinter sliding out. Immediately a childhood memory came to mind.

When I was about seven years old I was swinging about on a wooden gate when I got a huge splinter in the palm of my hand. I remember so well the shock, the pain and the awful realisation that somehow it couldn't stay embedded there and would have to come out! But in my terror I couldn't bear the thought and ran into the garden shed, locking myself in. I have a vivid memory of my mother trying to coax me out of the shed, first with soothing words, then with the promise of a Cornish strawberry Mivi, the most delicious ice lolly around at the time!

I explained this memory to the girl who had the picture and as she prayed for me, I saw in my mind an image of that splinter wedged deep into my broken heart, holding the two pieces together. That revelation made me realise that I had to ask someone to pray further as I had shut myself in a 'shed' for years because the thought of removing the splinter was so painful, and even the lure and promise of ice cream couldn't tempt me out this time! I saw that every time Georgie told me she was in pain, suffering or unhappy, the splinter pierced a bit deeper, stopping the flow of blood through the heart until the pain was so bad I just felt numb. But at least the splinter plugged the wound and held the pieces together. Still, clearly God wanted to remove that splinter and heal the wound, restoring my broken heart to wholeness.

I went to Bishop Peter Lee who was leading the house-party and, along with my friend Sally, he prayed for me. I seemed to be able to half open the shed door at first but I was too afraid of the pain to relinquish my hiding-place. I tried to imagine Jesus with his loving, healing arms waiting outside to soothe the wound and in prayer I saw the protective shed burned down forever. Next the splinter had to be dealt with. I tried hard to pull it out but the barbs clung to the flesh and pulled it back in until the pain was so intense I could hardly function. And now there was nowhere to run and hide. I was left knowing that I was wounded but unable to save myself. This, I realised months later at Burrswood, was the beginning of the crisis of faith which now brought me to such despair. The splinter had to be removed, somehow, once and for all, or I would certainly bleed to death.

Back at Burrswood, as Pat and Steve prayed with me, I was able to see all those vicious barbs so clearly – and how many there were! So much grief unexpressed, so much anger untold, so many years lost, so many images scarred on my memory. I had thought I had coped, been strong, endured it all so bravely – and in a way I *had* borne it with courage perhaps. I tried to understand that each one of those barbs was on the crown of thorns that Jesus wore, and all that pain had been suffered and nailed forever to his cross so that I didn't have to carry the pain any longer. But I struggled to believe that Jesus could reach down into this pain with his healing. Prayer seemed meaningless. As I write this now, I almost feel the need to apologise for such a time, but I tell this in honesty in the hope that it might help someone else.

Mercifully, though I had given up on me, others hadn't. They encouraged me to keep on praying even if it didn't seem to make sense. A passage from the writings of Julian of Norwich spoke to me:

So He says this, 'Pray inwardly, even though you find no joy in it. For it does you good, though you feel nothing, see nothing, yes, even though you think you cannot pray. For when you are dry and empty, sick and weak, your prayers please me, though there be little enough to please you.'

And later she wrote:

He says, 'Do not blame yourself too much, thinking that your trouble and distress is all your fault. For it is not my will that you should be unduly sad and despondent.'
Our enemy tries to depress us by false fears which he proposes. His intention is to make us so weary and dejected that we let the blessed sight of our everlasting friend slip from our minds.

It summed me up and I felt defeated. The blessed sight of my everlasting friend had slipped away and left me searching for him in vain. It wasn't that I had stopped believing in God intellectually. It seemed as reasonable as it had ever done to me to acknowledge a Creator. It wasn't even that I couldn't accept that he might be a loving God – in the abstract. But I felt totally unable to see him, to respond or trust that he loved me personally or that I could have any confidence that he had a plan and purpose to bless and care for me. Yes, I knew that I was in desperate need of inner healing, that the splinter would choke my life until I could no longer carry on, but I had lost hope that he could reach down to me – or even that he was bothered. I tried to summon up the old feelings, endeavoured to drum up faith within me by remembering old hymns and prayers:

> Fight the good fight with all thy might
> Christ is thy strength and Christ thy right
> Lay hold on life and it shall be
> Thy joy and crown eternally.
>
> John Samuel Bewley Monsell

'But I've lost my *might*!' I wailed. 'How can you lay hold on life when you've lost all your might?'

Frantically I tried to claw my way out of this hole. Striving, effort, longing, I agonised continually over my failure to resolve this crisis. As Mimi and Georgie pointed out, I was probably having a crisis of faith and they insisted on calling me 'Catherine Crisis' for many months. (When the sun *finally* shone again they renamed me 'Rachel Revived'!) Eventually, it was Steve who put a question to me which halted me in all my flailing.

'Are you willing to stay in the pit and just catch glimpses of God? Could you stay in this hollow darkness and simply wait for him to lift you out rather than perpetually trying to scramble up the rough sides of the crumbling hole you are in?'

My face fell as he gently put these questions to me. What on earth was he saying? Was God actually wanting me to *rest* in this place of solitude and despair? What about all the prayers to 'banish the darkness, dispel the gloom and ride triumphant to victory' that I felt I should be saying? Could it actually be possible that this feeling of separation and abandonment, this crisis of faith, was a *good* thing? A friend had written me a card with the words:

'*For your faithful people, Lord, life is changed not taken away.*' Yet these words had an empty ring to them for me as I viewed them from the bottom up, so to speak. Without the familiar closeness of God, life felt as if it *had* been taken away; there seemed no point and no purpose. I was hollow inside, an empty shell. Steve continued with his theme and encouraged me by saying, 'Rest in God's presence. Don't pull away. Wait . . . Even empty shells can be useful.'

A friend, Kitty, recommended a book, quite unaware that I was having this crisis. Called *Adam, God's Beloved*, it was completed only weeks before the death of its author, Henri Nouwen, and tells of his experience of sharing his life with people with mental disabilities as pastor of the L'Arche Daybreak Community in Toronto, Canada, and in particular about his extraordinary friendship with his severely disabled friend, Adam, whom he cared for for many years. Quite apart from the deep understanding about God which Nouwen learnt from the witness of his friend's life and suffering, he writes of the revelation of his own enormous spiritual and emotional emptiness. I devoured the account with numbness, yet hearing, in his broken, tender descriptions, an echo of my own sad soul.

Towards the end of 1987 I realised that I was heading for a crisis. I wasn't sleeping well . . . it was as if the planks that had covered my emotional abyss had been taken away and I was looking into a canyon full of wild animals waiting to devour me. I found myself overwhelmed by intense feelings of abandonment, rejection, neediness, dependence and despair. Here I was in the most peaceful house, with the most peaceful people, but raging inside myself . . . I soon found myself speaking to a psychiatrist. Everyone said the same thing. 'It is time for you to face your demons. It is time to bind your own wounds, to let others care for you.' It was a very humbling proposal. I had to leave the community for a place where I could live through my anguish in the hope of finding new strength and peace . . . I had to fully acknowledge my own disabilities.

I was going through the deep human struggle to believe in my own belovedness even when I had nothing to be proud of. Yes, I had left university with its prestige, but this life gave me satisfaction and even brought admiration. Yes, I was considered a good, even noble person because I was helping the poor! But now the last crutch had been taken away, I was challenged to believe that even when I had nothing to show for myself, I was still God's beloved son.

As I lived through this emotional ordeal I realised that I was becoming like Adam [my friend]. He had nothing to be proud of. Neither had I. He was completely empty. So was I. He needed full-time attention. So did I . . . yet I did not want to be dependent and weak. I did not want to be so needy. Somewhere though I recognised the way of radical vulnerability was also the way of Jesus.

During the months that I spent away I was able – with much guidance – to hear a soft and gentle inner voice saying, 'You are my beloved child, on you my favour rests.' For a long time I distrusted that voice. I kept saying to myself, 'It is a lie. I know the truth. There is nothing in me worth loving.'

It took some time for Henri Nouwen to believe that inner voice and to put his trust in those words, but eventually he did and returned to the community where he realised that his weak and dying friend had opened his heart to the 'gift of vulnerability'.

In our society plagued by fear, anxiety, loneliness, depression, and a sense of being lost, we keep looking for guides. We so much hope that someone – a guru, spiritual director, or soul friend – can help us make sense out of our confusion and can show us a way to inner wholeness, freedom and peace. We look mostly for men and women with a reputation, with wisdom, psychological insight, spiritual sensitivity, and solid life experience. Perhaps the problem is that we expect too much and they want to give us too much. Then we become dependent and they become controlling . . . Adam was the least controlling and the most dependent guide I ever encountered . . . In his total powerlessness Adam was a pure instrument of God's healing power . . . for me.

Nouwen went on to explore this idea of the fulfilment of God's will in our powerlessness:

The word '*passion*' is derived from the Latin verb '*patior*' which means '*to undergo*'. It is related to the word '*passive*'.

Jesus' passion came after much action. For three years he went from village to village, town to town, preaching, teaching, responding to people's questions, healing the sick, confronting the hypocrites, consoling the sorrowing, calling the dead back to life. Wherever he went there were large crowds of people admiring him, listening to him, asking him for help. During those intense, hectic three years Jesus was in control of the situation. He came and went as he felt it was right for him to do. His disciples accepted his leadership and followed him wherever he went.

But at Gethsemane – the Garden of Olives – all this action came to a sudden end. There Jesus was handed over by one of his own disciples to undergo suffering. That's where his passion began. From that moment he could no longer *do* anything; everything was done to him. He was arrested, put in prison, led before Herod and Pilate, flagellated, crowned with thorns, given a cross to carry, and ridiculed until he died. He could no longer act. It was pure passion.

The great mystery of Jesus' life is that he fulfilled his mission not in action but in passion, not by what he did but by what was done to him, not by his own decision but by other people's decisions concerning him. It was when he was dying on the cross that he cried out, 'It is fulfilled.'

And Nouwen's conclusion really caught my eye:

The truth is that a very large, if not the largest part of our lives is passion. Although we all want to act on our own, be independent and self-sufficient, we are for long periods of time dependent on other people's decisions. Not only when we are young and in-experienced or when we are old and needy but also when we are strong and self-reliant. Substantial parts of our success, wealth, health and relationships are influenced by events and circumstances over which we have little or no control. We like to keep up the illusion of action as long as we can, but the fact is that passion is what finally determines the course of our life. We need people, loving and caring people, to sustain us during the time of our passion and thus support us to accomplish our mission. That, to me is the final significance of Adam's passion: a radical call to accept the truth of our lives and to choose to give our love when we are strong and to receive the love of others when we are weak, always with tranquillity and generosity.

So there it was, a whisper of peace into my weary, broken heart. No more struggling and fighting to prove my strength and faithfulness. I had to be prepared to accept my vulnerability and weakness, to take the path of passion, not action, to receive the love of God and of others because of their grace, not my acceptability. After three 'intense . . . hectic years' when I had sought to stay in control, to keep on being strong, to remain coping, I was now sharing in the mystery of Jesus's passion. Suddenly I saw why Nouwen described it as a 'gift' of vulnerability. Precious indeed to be identified with Christ in the redemptive mystery of his suffering, death and resurrection. I would never have thought to choose the darkness and despair, but in it I saw there could be a closeness to *his* tender, loving heart which I might never otherwise have discovered. 'The way of radical vulnerability was also the way of Jesus.'

13

One thing I ask
One thing I seek
That I may dwell
In your house, O Lord
All of my days, all of my life,
That I may see you, Lord.

Hear me, O Lord, hear me when I cry.
Lord, do not hide your face from me.
You have been my strength
You have been my shield
And you will lift me up.

Song by Andy Park
Vineyard Music

It is a strange fact that we are often most strong when
people think we are vulnerable and most vulnerable when

people think we are strong. In the heat of battle we rise to heights of courage we would never have thought possible; when the fight subsides our guard is dropped and we are far more open to attack. Our own weakness and need had been all too apparent for three years and yet during all those frightening months and experiences we had always felt upheld and strengthened by the love and prayers of others, resolved to fight and never admit defeat. Now our situation seemed less desperate but in many ways we had never been more in need.

Georgie had grown significantly, thanks to the growth injections, and had also filled out a bit. Her hair had been styled into an attractive short crop and people started to remark on how well she looked. Music to our ears in one way, but ironically her very improvement produced a kind of wall between me and the outside world. While Georgie had been physically and obviously ill, there had been immediate sympathy and understanding from all who met her. Now that she *looked* 'normal', everyone just expressed relief and joy that it was 'all over'. How could I explain that in many ways we were still fighting giants and monsters? How could I point out that the pain of chronic fatigue was real and terrible even though it couldn't be put in a plaster cast? How could Georgie describe the night-mares that still haunted her troubled sleep and the weariness which accompanied every waking moment? Everyone wanted to believe their prayers had been an-swered and everything was going to be all right, so it was very hard to reply to the cheerful, bright comments, 'Well, actually things are still really difficult. Please keep praying for us and supporting us.'

With my mind I kept telling myself that I was sharing

in Christ's suffering as he was sharing in mine. His strength made perfect in my weakness? His grace sufficient for me? Try as I might, these comforting ideas remained only in my head, not in my heart. I felt extraordinarily alone. And dead. I was losing track of the days and the seasons. My own identity seemed to have blurred and diminished. I was an extension of Georgie's needs, a function of her illness, and the boundaries of my existence seemed limited by the four walls of my home. I felt interpreted by my role as a carer and my worth evaluated by my ability to alleviate my daughter's suffering and invest her with the will to live and fight. But I had lost mine.

No one except my immediate family and the staff at Burrswood realised the blackness into which I had descended during this time. Depression, grief, mental illness, I'm not sure what label best fits the terrible sense of loss and mourning I experienced for many months. All might have been lost but for one particular event which opened a chink of light on the desperate darkness that encompassed me.

I was driving past a field ablaze with sunflowers when suddenly into my mind flashed a picture of a large capsule. It was made of grey metal and was enclosed, a bit like a tomb, a stark contrast to the riot of colour and brightness of the sunflowers. Its ominous form suggested sinister secrets and I was troubled as to what was inside and its significance in my life. But it wasn't until I was praying later with Pat at Burrswood that the tomb revealed its ghastly contents.

It was indeed a place of death. Death of hope, death of career, death of faith, death of joy, death of trust. The graveyard of all my dreams. The floor of the tomb was littered with dirty rags, bones and vomit. The stench was terrible. I was appalled to see the charnel house my life had become. Now surely the only thing I had left was my own physical life and how I longed now to lay it down and be free at last from the horror of this living mortuary.

> O the mind, mind has mountains; cliffs of fall
> Frightful, sheer, no-man-fathomed. Hold them cheap
>> May who ne'er hung there.

The dreadful path of my journey now led through the dark landscape of my mind. Again and again I called out to a God who seemed to have removed all sense of his presence:

> And my lament
> Is cries countless, cries like dead letters sent
>> To dearest him that lives alas! away.

No answer. No comfort. No light.

> I cast for comfort I can no more get
> By groping round my comfortless, than blind
>> Eyes in their dark can day or thirst can find
>> Thirst's all-in-all in all a world of wet.

The old school copy of Gerard Manley Hopkins' poems revealed a voice which poured out all the longing and anguish of my heart. A sense of desolation, the human, shuddering recoil from the strain of rigorous discipline – a sourness, loss of hope, of joy, almost a suspension of faith itself which makes the victim feel that he is totally separated from his God. Yet as I read once more these desperate sonnets I discovered not self-pity but ultimately an heroic acceptance and willing self-surrender to the inscrutable compassion of God:

> In a flash, at a trumpet crash,
> I am all at once what Christ is, since he was what I
>   am, and
> This Jack, joke, poor potsherd, patch, matchwood,
>   immortal diamond,
>   Is immortal diamond.

This anguished Jesuit priest writing more than a hundred years ago taught me patience. It is we who reproach ourselves, not God. Broken, helpless, abandoned, Christ was all those things and still in the centre of his Father's will. Dead, defeated, deserted he appeared, yet in truth only waiting, waiting for God's time to roll back the stone and flood the tomb with light. I had to learn to be kinder to myself, to love the life which had cost God's Son his own.

> My own heart let me more have pity on; let
>   Me live to my sad self hereafter kind,
>   Charitable; not live this tormented mind
> With this tormented mind tormenting yet . . .
> Soul, self; come, poor Jackself, I do advise
> You, jaded, let be; call off thoughts awhile
>   Elsewhere; leave comfort root-room; let joy size
> At God knows when to God knows what; whose
>   smile

's not wrung, see you, unforeseen times rather – as
skies
    Betweenpie mountains – lights a lovely mile.

Jesus stood at the mouth of Lazarus's tomb and called for
death to give up its prisoner. At Burrswood the same
prayer began to draw me out of the darkness. A ray of
light shone into my living tomb and in that faint glimmer
the symbols of all my loss and grief began to shrivel and
disappear. Gradually, slowly, over the next few weeks the
light reached further and further into the darkest corners
and despair gave way to tender hope. The splinter was
drawn out of my heart so gently and each wound was
washed with the water of his love. I saw that like a
newborn kitten, blind and weak, I had not been able
to lift up my head to the light, but even in the darkness
sustenance had come and now my eyes were being
opened.

'Our eyes look to the Lord, till he shows us his mercy.'
These words from Psalm 123 had a new meaning for me.
I had thought because God had appeared to be looking
away he had ceased to care or think of me. But I realised
that a baby is no less loved just because the mother turns
to attend to the needs of her other children. The baby has
not been forgotten or abandoned. I have watched a baby
follow his mother's every movement round the room and
gaze fixedly at the door if she goes out for a moment, but
never cry. He is confident that she has always returned,
always met his needs, always held him in her heart and,
when he cries, ultimately, gloriously, in her arms. I
remembered the picture of the dog who gave up and
died because it thought its master had looked away and

ceased to care. But now I saw that dog had a beautiful, new, red collar and lead which was firmly held by the master. The link, the safety line, the guide rope, the restraint, the bond and mark of ownership were clearly visible. Not abandoned, never deserted, always belonging, ever loved. I would sit and wait patiently at the Master's feet, for however long it took, looking to him until he showed me his mercy.

I made a crown of thorns once. My mother showed me how to do it, wearing thick gardening gloves, yet still the barbs pierced my hands and fingers. We were making it to put around the crucifix on the altar for the Good Friday service. The chaplet of thorns had a vivid sense of contrast about it: on the one hand I had blood from its cruel snags yet on the other it seemed to represent humility and sacrifice. Even the protection of thick, suede-covered gauntlets couldn't mask the sense of shame that filled my heart. How *could* we have put this on his head? How can love be so deeply expressed through pain? I needed to touch each sharp point around the crown just to feel what it must have been like. I could control whether the barb pierced my skin; he could not.

As I tried to weave the thorns into a crown my hands felt clumsy and useless in the thick gloves. I couldn't bend the stem and hold it at the same time. It kept popping undone. A length of florist's wire did the trick in the end but it needed two of us: one to hold, the other to mould. I remembered this incident when I read this verse in Job: 'He is wooing you from the jaws of distress' (Job 36:16).

God's arms may encircle and hold us in difficult times but without the help of friends, family, ministers, doctors, nurses, intercessors and many unknown faithful people who pray and mould the situation with their skill, love and prayers, we may feel that we will bleed to death from the sharp barbs of our circumstances, the pain which threatens to swallow us. Many people feel they do not have earthly arms to woo them from the jaws of distress. They are being eaten alive with little comfort or relief. They may not feel there is any protection from the relentless, sharp thorns of depression and worthlessness. Often they shun the help of others, not wanting to reveal their inner ugliness. But the everlasting arms are there to encircle all of us, and admission of our helplessness is often the first step in realising we are not as alone as we first thought. Our need is not always readily perceived but we must try to find the humility and trust to ask for the help that will turn the twisted crown of sharp thorns into a circle of love. The strands of prayers can hold us more tightly than any florist's wire could. We still can't control how and when the thorns will pierce our flesh but the arms of grace, both heavenly and earthly, can ease the pain a little.

There can be hope for the future. In a magazine recently, a film star discussed a very difficult time in her life and commented, 'Even when you're sad, lonely or depressed for a time, even when you feel the world is not being kind to you, something inside you can resist being destructive and hold out for happiness again.' We are not alone. As we try to endure and persevere through the pain we are always held. God's arms surround us. Sometimes we feel the pressure of his embrace, can almost hear the beat of his loving heart; at other times he appears to bear us so lightly that we fear we have been allowed to fall. But it is never so. 'He gathers the lambs in his arms and carries them close to his heart' (Isaiah 40:11). When we are too weak to continue, he carries us. This is not failure but grace. It is the wonderful truth expressed in the famous 'Footprints' piece:

One night a man had a dream. He dreamed he was walking along the beach with the Lord. Across the sky flashed scenes from his life. For each scene he noticed two sets of footprints in the sand: one belonging to him and the other to the Lord.

When the last scene of his life flashed before him, he looked back at the footprints in the sand. He noticed that many times along the path of his life there was only one set of footprints. He also noticed that it happened at the very lowest and saddest times in his life.

This really bothered him and he questioned the Lord about it. 'Lord, you said that once I decided to follow you, you'd walk with me all the way. But I have noticed that during the most troublesome times in my life, there is only one set of footprints. I don't understand why when I needed you most you would leave me.'

The Lord replied, 'My precious child, I love you and would never leave you. During your times of trial and suffering, when you see only one set of footprints, it was then that I carried you.'

Author unknown

14

*In a desert land he found him, in a barren and howling
waste. He shielded him and cared for him; he guarded
him as the apple of his eye.*

Deuteronomy 32:10

There is a painting by Rembrandt of the return of the
prodigal son. It is a picture suffused with great sorrow and
great joy. The focal point is the hands of the father laid in
blessing and forgiveness on the broken form of his lost
son. A warm, tender light falls on the embrace which seeks
to raise and restore, to draw close and love. The expression
on the face of the father is one of ineffable compassion.

I have thought long about that embrace. The father is
holding out his arms to the son, extending forgiveness and
healing. What will be the response of the son? Will he
remain, abject and humiliated, on the ground, or will he

rise to meet the love which forgets its hurt and rejection and extends the offer of acceptance and protection? We know from the story that the father calls a banquet to celebrate the son's return so we can assume that the son reciprocates in gratitude and love.

I have come to understand a little of the heavenly embrace which is always extended to us but I have also reflected on the need for us to respond to human embrace, not just physically but spiritually. Bishop Peter Lee, summarising a more extended treatment by Miroslav Volf in his book *Exclusion and Embrace*, identifies four stages of embrace:

1. *In me.* I must make the decision to open myself up, to unfold my arms. For some of us it is not so much that there is no one to hug us, but that we are too fearful of hurting to open ourselves up either literally or metaphorically. We have been let down, disappointed, even betrayed. Just as in a marriage when trust has been lost, we are frightened that to embrace will only open raw wounds and bring new pain. It takes enormous courage and faith sometimes to take that step forward and expose your bruised heart. But without human and divine embrace, hope and love will wither and die.

2. *In the other person.* It is difficult to embrace someone who has turned the other way, refuses to open his arms or is trying to walk off. The other person has decisions to make, whether to engage in that union by unfolding their arms, or to remain aloof, alone.

3. *It is reciprocal.* An embrace is mutual. It involves four arms. The host becomes the guest and the guest becomes the host. An embrace is meaningless unless the recipient responds. Then there is an unbroken circle of love which conveys reassurance and commitment.

4. *Let go!* You cannot live in a constant embrace. Nothing would ever get done if we walked around hugging each other the whole time. We need to let go of the embrace to be able to continue life and release the other person to go their way. It is fear, again, which makes it difficult to let go. We are scared that without that emotional support we will not be able to cope, or worse, that if the embrace is over so will be the love.

Finally the picture reminds me that he is the God of the second chance. The father in the story had already given his son everything – and had been repaid with the deepest insult and rejection. Yet he was prepared and longing to pour out still more symbols of his love and forgiveness – and ready to do that even before the prodigal son had uttered any words of repentance. He was looking, waiting, hoping for the opportunity to embrace and give his son a second chance.

It fascinates me that the prodigal son did have the courage to return to his father. He had treated his father with the greatest disdain. To ask for his inheritance early was tantamount to wishing that his father was dead, a gross insult. Yet his father didn't cuff him round the ears and strike him out of his will immediately but complied with his selfish, ill-advised request, making himself the poorer thereby. What gave the son the right to feel he would be forgiven and accepted if he returned? I have a feeling that quite apart from what the son might have known about his father's kindness, there must have been an element of desperation about his decision. He couldn't get any lower than eating the pigs' scraps, the leftover swill from animals considered unclean and profane to the Jews. Where else could he go? Who would have him now he was so abased? Outcast and abandoned, he would surely die anyway. Better at least to see his father once more and, if rejected, to die in his own country and not among strangers.

Nowhere else to go. The disciple Peter knew that only Jesus had the words of eternal life. If he turned his back on Jesus there was no one else who could save him. That is why his grief over his denial was even more poignant, he had not only betrayed his master and friend but almost lost all his faith and hope. The abyss into which he stared was too dreadful to contemplate and he rededicated his life to Christ with a vehemence which enabled him to suffer a fearful execution.

Job echoed the cry of heart-wrung faith: 'Though he slay me, yet will I hope in him' (Job 13:15). It was the same last-ditch trust that gave Daniel and his friends their extraordinary courage when King Nebuchadnezzar threatened to throw them in the blazing furnace if they didn't bow down and worship the golden image he had made.

> 'O Nebuchadnezzar,' [declared Daniel] 'we do not need to defend ourselves before you in this matter. If we are thrown into the blazing furnace, the God we

serve is able to save us from it, and he will rescue us from your hand, O king. But even if he does not, we want you to know, O king, that we will not serve your gods or worship the image of gold you have set up.'

Daniel 3:16–18

'But even if he does not.' 'Whither shall I go, Lord?' 'Though he slay me . . .' For more than two thousand years, people of faith have realised that even though God's ways may be incomprehensible, even though he may not appear to answer, even if they have to conclude that he doesn't seem to care, *they will not give up*. They will turn away from despair and self-destruction and choose to trust – to trust blindly perhaps, but we all see through a darkened glass – to trust, endure and persevere to whatever end there might be.

But some do not. Cannot. During these years of enduring and sharing in suffering, I have seen examples of unbelievable courage. People who have kept the faith even though they have been repeatedly knocked down, when the heavens have seemed like brass, even when their hopes and prayers have ended at the graveside. But I have seen others broken on the rack of endless pain, or destroyed by the onslaught of depression or grief. What makes the difference? Is it personality, spirituality, circumstances or chance? Is there anything we can learn from those who have persevered through terrible suffering to enable us to keep our foothold on the slippery mountain slope above the abyss and turn our faces to the light? I began to talk to people who were struggling through pain and sorrow to see if there was any comfort or encouragement I might draw together to offer a rope, a hand in the darkness, to those stumbling towards the edge.

Faced with an unbearable situation, two men will react in very different ways. The television presenter, Clive James, used to host an awful but compelling programme in which young Japanese men would endure the most horrible 'games'. To win, the contestants went through ordeal after ordeal involving spiders, frogs, worms, being blindfolded and eating unmentionable delicacies, being submerged in tanks filled with 'lethal' sea snakes, and many other extraordinarily disgusting or gruesome challenges. The idea was to endure at all costs. The winner, or rather the hero as he became, was the man who put up with the most humiliation, pain and degradation – or had the strongest stomach!

Quite a different game was played in the Second World War. On Christmas Day 1941, Stanley Maughan, a neighbour of ours, was taken prisoner in Hong Kong. He was one week short of celebrating his twenty-sixth birthday and was serving as a member of the Hong Kong Volunteer Defence Corps. For the following four years Stanley was interned as a POW and finally came out after VJ Day in September 1945.

There were five thousand men in the camp and part of the daily regime involved all those prisoners being hauled out of the barracks to line up and be counted. There was a road running down the centre of the barracks and the men had to stand on the pavement for *bango*, the Japanese word for 'number'. Stanley remembers the hours of waiting aimlessly while all the prisoners were accounted for.

One particular incident has stayed with him all his life. Stanley was standing in line next to a man slightly older than himself who had been a don at Oxford and had then been recruited for the Colonial Office. From their snatches of conversation, Stanley saw this young man was very learned and bright, and had obviously been a real scholar. But suddenly something extremely bizarre happened.

'This fellow turned to me,' Stanley recalled, 'and he said, "I'm fed up with this." And with that he sat down on the pavement and died at my feet. I was amazed and shocked. I didn't know you could just sit down and die.'

Recently Stanley attended a lunch for POW survivors and as he looked round the room he wondered how they had all got through and survived. He observed that they all appeared to be *joyful* people. He thinks they survived *because* of that inner strength and that possibly the less positive ones, the ones who tended to look on the black side of life, couldn't survive. But he also made the observation that he managed to endure the horrors of the camp partly because of his lack of analysis and questioning of his situation:

It was bloody awful but you just got on with it. I persevered through plain ignorance. If I had been more sensitive I would have been more worried and depressed. But I didn't think the war would last more than six months. You see, I was a colonial and very proud of the British Empire so I just couldn't believe that the Japs had it in them to last more than six months and that kept me going. But then the six months turned into four years and then I had to rely on what I'd been taught in Sunday school, 'Live for the day and don't worry about tomorrow', and I think that's what I did, just went on day by day.

His 'day by day' meant latrine-cleaning. There had been an epidemic of dysentery, a quite terrible thought with a camp of five thousand men, and Stanley *volunteered* to muck out the latrines. There were 'dry latrines' with a foot of sludge, overflowing pans and the most foul stench imaginable, and it was into this that Stanley, with rolled-up trousers and bare feet, would wade to fill the buckets and empty the excrement into the sea – under armed guard. He says he got used to it. Somehow he got used to it. He endured his appalling task though he says now that he would be utterly sick if he had to do something like that today!

But Stanley has survived. He was eighty-four on the night the world welcomed a new millennium, celebrating it with his wife, children and grandchildren, having lived a very full and interesting life despite being registered blind as a result of beriberi contracted when he was a POW. One of the many unsung heroes of the war.

Take a day at a time. This is the first and perhaps most important thought I have drawn from my own experience and from others. My sister Annie advised, 'Don't borrow sorrow from tomorrow.' It is hard enough to find strength to bear today's burden of suffering without worrying whether tomorrow will bring more and whether we will cope. Sufficient for the day are the evils thereof. Tomorrow may indeed bring fresh pain or setback, but that's not to say that grace and divine help might not abound even more. Or if they don't, that courage won't rise to meet the new fight.

The second observation is that a cheerful heart really does promote healing and hope. I'm not talking about a flippant, superficial, happy-clappy self-delusion ('I know I look utterly miserable but I'm really rejoicing underneath') nor the world's recipe for spiritual fulfilment which lies in self-assertion and positive thinking: 'Demand your rights, reclaim your will! Life is tough; be tougher!' I personally feel that both these approaches lead ultimately to exhaustion and failure because both rely on the strength and endurance of the individual alone. Neither of them can accept the reality of depression or chronic pain which can make buoyancy of emotions an impossibility for a time. I think a cheerful heart is more akin to a calm acceptance and rest accompanied by an appreciation of the beauty or pleasure in the smallest object or act. The Bible encourages us to 'give thanks *in* all circumstances' (1 Thessalonians 5:18), not *because of* all circumstances.

I'm also struck that the Bible talks about joy but not happiness, and I wonder if God is not able to uplift our spirit even though our feelings may be cast down. Jesus was a man of sorrows, acquainted with grief, yet I'm certain that he imparted joy to all who were near him. Children always suss out hypocrisy or insincerity and they adored him. From all the suffering of the past years, I have come to believe there is a still, quiet place at the centre of all our pain where we can find the Spirit of God lifting up our head and turning us away from despair. Even when our heart is breaking we can know his voice urging us to live and hope again. And by his grace it is possible to respond. This is real heroism, I believe. It is in the quiet, continuing fight, the refusal to succumb to the darkness, the whisper that says, 'I don't understand you but I trust you.'

15

'There is no other way to survive except to be in the moment.'

Christopher Reeve

Hero: a name given to men of superhuman strength, courage or ability, favoured by the gods;

a man distinguished by extraordinary valour and martial achievements; one who does brave or noble deeds; an illustrious warrior;

a man who exhibits extraordinary bravery, firmness, fortitude or greatness of soul in any course of action or in connection with any pursuit, work or enterprise; a man admired and venerated for his achievements and noble qualities.

The Oxford English Dictionary

I feel uncomfortable when people describe our reactions to the difficulties of the past few years as 'heroic' or brave. Given the textbook definition, nothing could be further from the truth. I have always imagined a hero to be someone of obvious moral and spiritual superiority, a really strong, dynamic personality who was just waiting for the opportunity to flex his pectorals. Superman is the archetype, and it was shocking and incomprehensible to hear in 1995 that the real Superman, Christopher Reeve, had been left paralysed from the neck down after a riding accident. I often wondered how he coped with the cataclysmic end to his health and career, and was moved by the account of his suffering and endurance in his autobiography *Still Me*:

> My wife Dana and I finally reached a conclusion that we could both accept – that God doesn't make these things happen. We are given free will, and everything obeys the laws of nature. If you are flung over a horse's head you may very well break your neck. It just happens. But where God comes in, where grace enters, is in the strength you find to deal with it. You may not know where it comes from, but there's an enormous power at work.

He then describes how his understanding of what it meant to be a hero had changed:

> When the first Superman movie came out, I gave dozens of interviews to promote it. The most frequently asked question was: 'What is a hero?' I remember how easily I'd talk about it, the glib

response I repeated so many times. My answer was that a hero is someone who commits a courageous action without considering the consequences. A soldier who crawls out of a foxhole to drag an injured buddy back to safety, the prisoners of war who never stop trying to escape even though they know they may be executed if they're caught. And I also meant individuals who are slightly larger than life: Houdini and Lindbergh, John Wayne and JFK and even sports figures who have taken on mythical proportions.

Now my definition is completely different. *I think a hero is an ordinary individual who finds the strength to persevere and endure in spite of overwhelming obstacles . . . These are the real heroes, and so are the family and friends who have stood by them.*

He concludes:

There is no other way to survive except to be in the moment. Just as my accident and its aftermath caused me to redefine what a hero is, I've had to take a hard look at what it means to live as fully as possible in the present.

As I read and talk to people about their experience of suffering, this same theme keeps recurring: there is no glory or public recognition in coping with relentless trials or constant pain; only the hard graft of desperate endurance and gritty perseverance enables us to cope. No one feels proud or triumphant. You just 'get on with it', try to deal with the day ahead.

Charles Spurgeon, the outstanding nineteenth-century preacher and writer, understood only too well the darkness of suffering. From the time he came to his London pulpit at nineteen, he was the butt of cruel jokes in the press and the object of scorn from other clergy. Depression was a frequent and exhausting companion. He suffered from gout, a disease that produces dreadful misery, and pain hounded him during the last twenty years of his life. His wife, Susannah, became an invalid at thirty-three and could seldom attend church to hear her husband preach. Yet, among the concluding words of what, unknown to him, was his final sermon, Spurgeon testified of Christ:

He is the most magnanimous of captains . . . He is always to be found in the thickest part of the battle. When the wind blows cold, he always takes the bleakest side of the hill. The heaviest end of the cross lies ever on his shoulders. If he bids us carry a burden, he carries it also. If there is anything that is gracious, generous, kind and tender, yea lavish and supernatural in love, you always find it in him. These forty years and more have I served him, and I have nothing but love from him. I would be glad to continue another forty years in the same dear service here below, if it so pleased him. His service is life, peace, joy.

Despite times when he clearly felt deep depression, Spurgeon continued to preach this message of God's faithfulness. Six thousand people crowded into his congregation to hear him preach every Sunday. He preached to other gatherings, sometimes as many as ten times a week. His Sunday sermons were taken down by stenographers and printed throughout England. They were cabled to New York on Monday and reprinted in leading newspapers throughout the United States. In 1865 Spurgeon's sermons sold 25,000 copies a week. They were translated into more than twenty languages. Spurgeon occupied the same pulpit for forty years and did not preach himself dry. God created a bush that blazed with fire and yet was not consumed.

And all out of suffering, not comfort. Obviously he wasn't simply a *happy* person; he was often low in spirits yet, I suspect, strangely serene. He accepted his condition as being the means of drawing him closer to his master but he knew that only perseverance to the very end would gain him the crown:

> Perseverance is the badge of a true saint. The Christian life is both a beginning and a continuation in the ways of God for as long as life lasts. Napoleon said, 'Conquest has made me what I am, and conquest must maintain me.' It is the same with a Christian. Under God, dear saint of the Lord, conquest has made you what you are and conquest must sustain you. Your motto must be, 'Excelsior'. Only a true conqueror will continue until war's trumpet is silenced. Then the conqueror will be crowned.
>
> Therefore, perseverance is the target of our spiritual enemies. The world does not object to your being a Christian for a while, just as long as you cease your pilgrimage and settle down to buy a house in Vanity Fair.

The flesh also seeks to ensnare and prevent you from pressing on to glory. It tempts, 'It is weary work being a pilgrim. Come, give it up. Am I always to be humiliated? Give me at least a furlough from this ongoing warfare.'

Satan, too, will make fierce attacks on your perseverance. It will be the target for his arrows. He will try to hinder. He will insinuate that your perseverance is no good and that you need a rest. He will try to make you weary of suffering. He will whisper, 'Curse God and die' (Job 2:9). He will attack your steadfastness. 'What is the good of being so zealous? Be quiet like the rest. Sleep as others do.'

Wear your shield, Christian. Close your armour and cry mightily to God that, by His Spirit, you will endure to the end.

Morning and Evening, ed. Roy H. Clarke, Nelson Word Ltd

So endurance is not dependent on our personality? Is it not easier to get through difficult times if you are a naturally cheerful person? You would think it was quite an advantage to be an optimist and that suffering would not perhaps be such a burden if your instinct were to believe everything would turn out fine in the end. I've thought about the different ways people react to pain and trials and initially it seemed that certainly some types fared better. In trying to draw some conclusion, I've compared them to different materials reacting to the flame of a candle.

Wool burns quickly, spitting a little and curling away to nothing quite quickly. People of this temperament find themselves swiftly overwhelmed by adverse circumstances. Although they strive to fight against their circumstances, their faith and hope stutter in the attempt to hold on to life and they fade away.

Paper burns swiftly with a lot of flame and light but gives little heat, and is quickly extinguished. Such people, perhaps new in the faith, respond with great fervour to the first call to battle and appear to have incredible resilience, setting a fine example of courage and faith, but when the battle turns into trench warfare they lack the stamina to keep on going.

Leather gives off a singeing odour as it browns and curls at the edges, becoming hard and brittle before crumbling. People of this unemotional kind appear to withstand the heat of adversity well, outwardly enduring the difficulties with apparent fortitude, but underneath their hope is being subtly eroded as they rely on their own strength rather than resting in God's. Bitterness and cynicism may ultimately replace stoic perseverance.

Wood ignites fairly quickly, burns for some time and creates good light and heat, so intensely in fact that it is consumed entirely and turns to ash. Such extroverts are encouraging in their brave response to pressure and pain, inspiring others with their example, but their emotions are often on a rollercoaster and they desperately need support to continue as without it they eventually burn themselves out.

Coal takes a long time to catch fire and often needs some sort of kindling to get going. Once truly ignited it burns with an intense heat and for a long time but, again, cannot sustain the combustion alone. It moves to a glowing stage but quickly becomes a cold, grey shell if it falls out of the grate. More wary and fearful at first, introverts by temperament, these personalities can prove unexpectedly strong and courageous with the assurance of others and can appear to 'glow' throughout their suffering but, alone, succumb once more to self-doubt and questioning of their worth.

Metal doesn't burst into flame at all but just gets hotter and hotter as it transfers heat through its mass and starts to glow. In this pliable state it can be moulded and when melted down completely can be separated into its pure elements and the dross. This person's reaction to suffering is not so spectacular initially. There is no dramatic flame or instant heat. But in the long run, this type of faith produces the most sustained heat which warms others, adapts to the changing pressures of circumstances and finally itself becomes precious and beautiful and cherished.

So each personality type has its strengths and weaknesses. Each one of us reacts differently when 'the heat is on'. One is not any better nor worse than the next. Although in minor trials and difficulties certain temperaments undoubtedly find it easier to respond with faith and resist depression or fear, my experience is that in circumstances of sustained suffering the playing-field becomes much more level. In order to endure to the end we all need to become more like gold which is refined by fire, the dross being burnt away to reveal our weakness made perfect by his grace. Smith Wigglesworth, the inimitable preacher and writer, realised that the essential property of us all is changed by the fire of suffering and saw it as an opportunity for a closer fellowship with Christ:

The most trying time is the most helpful time. Most preachers say something about Daniel and about the Hebrew children, Shadrach, Meshach and Abednego, and especially about Moses when he was in a corner. Beloved, if you read the Scriptures, you will never find anything about the easy times. All the glories came out of the hard times.

And if you are to be really reconstructed, it will be in a hard time. It won't be in a singing meeting but at a time when you think all things are dried up, when you think there is no hope for you and you have passed up everything. That is the time that God makes the man. It is when you are tried by fire that God purges you, takes the dross away, and brings forth the pure gold. Only melted gold is minted. Only soft wax receives the seal. Only broken, contrite hearts receive the mark as the Potter turns us on His wheel, shaped and burned to take and keep the heavenly mould, the stamp of God's pure gold.

We must have the stamp of our blessed Lord who was marred more than any man. And when He touched human weakness, it was reconstructed. He spoke out of the depths of trial and mockery and became the Initiator of a world's redemption . . . He can take the weakest and make them into strength.

Smith Wigglesworth on Faith, Whitaker House, USA, 1998

16

For a brief moment I abandoned you, but with deep compassion I will bring you back.

Isaiah 54:7

It must be one of the oldest questions of the human race, Why does a loving God allow suffering? Even though in our own situation with Georgie some people like to try and give us answers, it's not a question we really bother asking now. Rather than asking, 'Why?' we might do better asking, 'Why not?'

We live in a broken world. At the centre of the chequered story of human survival on this earth stands a symbol of ultimate suffering and defeat, the cross. And on it, Christ gave up the peace, security and wholeness of his kingdom to bear our pain and our guilt. There's nothing we can tell him about the agony of betrayal, the terror of torture or the desolation of grief. He chose to experience the worst suffering and pain so that for eternity we might know that in whatever trials and sorrow we find ourselves, he has been there before us. There can be no agony like the sense of separation and rejection he voiced from the cross, his desolate cry encapsulating the anguish of the entire human race: 'My God, my God, why have you forsaken me?'

Yet if he had had the strength, he might have been heard, by those standing closest to the cross, whispering the words of trust found later in that psalm: 'I will declare your name to my brothers; in the congregation I will praise you . . . For he has not despised or disdained the suffering of the afflicted one; he has not hidden his face from him but has listened to his cry' (Psalm 22:22, 24).

In line with Jewish custom, after the agonising death of Jesus, the women spent many hours preparing precious spices and ointments to anoint his body. Mary and Mary Magdalene would have felt an overwhelming need to offer the poor broken body of their Lord the dignified symbols of cleansing and honour. How distraught they must have been to hear that a Roman guard had been posted outside the tomb, and a huge stone rolled over the mouth of the entrance. To be denied his body to weep over must have added to their grief. Yet, extraordinarily, on the Sabbath morning they still set off to the tomb bearing their precious gifts. Did they believe that miraculously the enormous stone would be rolled away? That the guard would politely let them in? Or could they simply not conceive of life without him? Despite every outward circumstance telling them that their faith and actions were in vain, they kept going, the dew-covered ground cool beneath their feet as they trudged on, exhausted by grief. Yet at the end of their journey, at the gate of death itself, they found mourning replaced by joy, darkness overcome by light, the stone of their despair rolled away to reveal the presence of the Lord himself.

I try to remember this when the obstacles seem insurmountable. The big stones are best left to him. He is the remover of rocks. It is not for me to try and push them aside. The boulders may seem solid with no possible way through, but the future is in his hands and he will hang lanterns in the darkness when the time comes to walk through the rubble.

So, questioning the past, seeking answers for the present and worrying about the future all rob us of our strength and peace. I almost called this book, 'Bitter, Batty or Better?' for that very reason. Once we have been robbed of our strength and peace, it is an easy road to becoming bitter about our situation, continually harping back to past events that have marred our happiness. For some it leads to breakdown. I think I know what it is to be quite close to that sense of madness taking over from normal reactions and feelings. But for others there can be the finding of something better. And perhaps we have to move through the first two to reach the last – emerge the other side a 'better' person, better for the experience, new growth springing from harsh pruning? Perhaps there is an element of choice about this too, for we can find ourselves frozen to the first step, refusing help to move onwards, frightened at the prospect of change; or sometimes too comfortable or too familiar with where we have got stuck. Taking one step at a time involves acceptance of the unknown, a willingness to remain in the darkness, trusting that glimpses of light will appear to lead us forward or, if not, that there will be a hand in the darkness.

Jenny Francis has endured many years of chronic pain and illness despite fervent prayer for healing. In her book *Belief beyond Pain*, she discusses the question of acceptance and explains that it is far from a cop-out:

> Acceptance is a term occasionally thrown to us by the medical profession: 'You'll have to learn to live with it. You'll just have to accept it – come to terms with it.' Some people misconstrue the word as meaning giving in, not trying any more, an opting out of conflict. It is not like that at all. To experience something akin to the bereaved as they work towards a new identity is to know what an enormous struggle it can be, quite the antithesis of opting out. For those apparently called to a life of severe pain, it seems an impossible prospect . . . True acceptance is a monumental step; it is hardly a light decision made on the spur of the moment. It often takes years and some never achieve it. They may remain too angry or resentful or sadly unable any longer to trust in a loving God who appears to remain aloof and does not draw alongside them in their distress . . .

> On bad days I feel totally unequal to the task of running the race that is set before me. A deep weariness pervades the hidden reaches of my soul and in my fatigue and weakness I can do nothing other than depend totally on God . . . It is in accepting my weakness so that I am wrapped in the Lord's love that I become strong, immensely

strong, girded by his power and love. I know that nothing can separate me from him. We have all heard these things before and we may cluck approvingly when someone testifies to such an experience, without reflecting how difficult it is to reach that point. It takes great courage to allow oneself to remain in such weakness, to be exposed, stripped naked in all sense before God. Bereft of clothes, layer upon layer of self stripped away to reveal a puny body and a more puny spirit, we find our feet placed on rock and know in our inmost being that it is God; he it is who wraps us in his love but does not necessarily exempt us from the world's evil . . .

When people meet great personal difficulties or tragedy, some find their very foundations shaken and in their distress wonder where God is. Sadly for some this leads to a lengthy estrangement or even complete severance from their belief. Others 'go the other way', as they say, and find comfort in religion. Perhaps there are times in our life's journey when we feel alienated from God and can only cling on to what we know intellectually, and it is as much as we can do to exercise a discipline of faith. This can be so painful yet somewhere in the recesses of the mind and heart we know we are not forgotten . . . There is always, even in the darkest reaches of my night, a slender golden thread somewhere which makes it bearable.

Jenny Francis, *Belief beyond Pain*, SPCK, 1992

Acceptance is constantly threatened by regrets and longings. I know I've said it often myself and I'm sure I've

Julie Sheldon

heard it many times from others too: 'If *only* I could get away from this pain just for a while'. To try and remember what it felt like to be pain-free and care-free is just the start of a ride on the seductive thought-train. It travels so fast that in no time at all it can lead to, and stop at, the two tiresome stations of 'If Only' and 'I Wish'. The station-master quickly ushers us in as we begin to dream and imagine the different scenarios: If only this hadn't happened. I wish I'd taken that advice. If only I hadn't taken that decision. If only . . . I wish . . . If only . . . I wish. The train continues its journey, rumbling on without us, as we are left behind, sitting cold and alone on the platform of reality. Bleakly we realise that the situation is not going to change and we have to 'come to terms with it'.

Personally I dislike that expression a lot. There is a ring of defeatism about it as if you have to accept that there will never be a return train and you will be stranded there forever. It suggests you should give in, lie back and give up hope. But true acceptance is not an admission of defeat. It is treading water rather than drowning. There may appear to be no progress but your head is above water and you're still breathing. Concentration is on maintaining your position rather than fighting against the current. A 'place of rest' is misleading as it implies that there is no effort involved, but in fact considerable energy may be expended in a focusing of thought, in meditation and prayer, rather than in a dissipation of reserves in frantic activity or worry.

Thoughts *can* be harnessed to provide an escape that is healthy and positive. When I was disabled with dystonia I longed, quite literally, to 'get out' of my body. I craved to

154

be transported from the intense pain and the contortions produced by the muscle spasms to a gentle, relaxed, quiet place where I could be free. Physically, though, I was bound to a disabled, decaying body and so I relied on my imagination to enable me to 'dance away'. I could imagine myself whirling, jumping, floating, not just on a stage but on the seashore, through the fields, on a windswept hillside. I could imagine it without bitterness. The real me, deep inside, was not broken and distorted, and in a positive way my thoughts could break the bounds of my illness.

Now, as a full-time 'carer', I long to see my daughter free from pain, enjoying her childhood again, being 'care-free' and also 'carer-free'! I can temporarily leave the home now and take a little time away from the illness but it's incredible how intense the reminders are when you get out 'into the world' of the limitations of your situation. The most acute, still, is seeing young children running and laughing in the playground. It feels like a bereavement, the grief at having lost that part of my daughter's childhood and personality. Sometimes it is uncomfortable to meet up with friends and hear of all the energetic sporting pursuits their children are getting up to. I share in their delight and understand their pride; it's just that, by contrast, our physical achievements seem so slow and limited.

It's vital, therefore, that we take whatever 'time out' we can to lift our spirits and renew our energy. This is a habit we should all adopt, whether or not our situation is one of acute or chronic distress. It doesn't take much to bring a more balanced perspective into our situation – a walk around our little village can help to calm my frayed nerves, a nod to a friend driving by in their car can make me realise I am not so isolated, and the sight of a family of moorhens bobbing about on the village pond can smooth away the frown lines better than any face-cream. As for Georgie, an outing to the post office to buy a magazine and a few sweeties can change the direction of the whole day. I think this is called the 'distraction technique' but whatever the technical term, there is definitely a need for respite through some form of temporary escape from the pressure of perseverance. If perseverance is like a hammer, endurance is the nail, one active, the other passive. Together they effect the join or the repair. But perpetual activity wears us down physically and mentally. We need to be aware that sometimes we should move aside from the effort of persevering, of consciously trying to press forward, and seek a quiet place of stillness and rest, a moment to enjoy the view from the peak instead of always chipping away at the hard rock of the bleak mountainside.

My friend Jill Lawson gave me a graphic illustration of this after taking part in a mission to the Blackpool area where they had been encouraged to take a little time off each day to get refreshed. Jill would go to the local indoor pool where it was possible not only to get a Senior Swim for just £1 but also a refund on her parking ticket!

On the day in question I had my swim and was enjoying a picnic lunch with thermos and sandwich. I had settled on a bench behind the sports centre, out of the wind, but after pouring out my drink I realised it was not the best choice of site. A decorative seaside lake had its backwater tucked behind this building, and because of the direction of the wind, this had become the repository for all kinds of rubbish. Old cans, polystyrene cups, twigs, leaves, scum – all had collected on the surface of the water. It would have needed a fine-meshed net and a willingness to get damp and smelly to clear the mess. Not only that, the side wall of the sports centre was a high, windowless area of angry red brick, unrelieved and uninspiring. This was my view.

I debated whether to pack up all my things and look for another spot but in the end I decided that it was too much bother to move to another bench and I would be bound to spill my coffee or lose a sandwich to the ducks. It was only when I gathered up my belongings after a rather depressing lunch and moved off that I realised what I had missed. Only a few feet along the promenade, the view was transformed! Instead of a murky backwater, the open lake danced and sparkled. There were fancy ducks, majestic swans and a large family of Canada geese, and beyond – the open sea, wind-whipped with white horses and a couple of sails on the distant horizon.

This seemed a picture of how easily, and how often, we can settle for second best when, with only a moment's resolve, we can move out of the safe but cheerless backwater, to a place where there is both sparkle and view.

This story spoke clearly to me. If we can just gather strength and take a few more steps, the depressing view of flotsam, jetsam, rubbish and scum could be exchanged for something much lighter, more inspiring and uplifting. For someone who is housebound through illness or through caring for someone ill, this might simply mean a drive in the car, a bunch of spring flowers, a dog to stroke, bringing the 'outside inside', anything to change the inward and downward view of being trapped in a difficult situation. I know of a little boy who, through illness, has spent virtually the last ten years in the same room. The same four walls. The same faces attending him. Very little colour touches his life. The curtains are drawn tight shut. The light hurts his eyes. His childhood has floated away as he has spent it on the murky backwater. What to do, what to say, how to help? I can only pray for Jesus to bring in his fine-meshed net. He doesn't mind getting wet and dirty if it means rescuing one of his children.

Not everyone is fortunate enough to have strong, constant support, and without it the task of daily endurance can sometimes seem overwhelming. The elderly, the very young and the disabled often feel isolated, neglected or misunderstood. If natural support of family or friends is lacking, we need to seek professional help if we possibly can and, indeed, usually need that as well. But in my experience, even Christian friends can get it wrong, and offer 'advice' that isn't necessarily the most helpful. This adaptation from *The Vision in the Valley* by Linda Richardson illustrates the point:

The Seventh Friend
When I was first diagnosed with cancer, my first friend came and expressed shock, saying, '*I can't believe that you have cancer. I always thought you were fit and healthy.*' He left and I felt alienated and somehow very different from everyone else.

My second friend came and brought me informa-

tion about treatments for cancer and said, '*Whatever
you do, don't take chemotherapy. It's a poison.*' She left
and I felt scared and confused.

My third friend came and tried to answer my
'whys' with the statement, '*Perhaps God is disciplin-
ing you for some sin in your life.*' He left and I felt
judged.

My fourth friend came and told me, '*If your faith
is great enough, God will heal you.*' She left and I felt
guilty.

My fifth came and told me to remember, '*All
things work together for good.*' He left and I felt angry.

My sixth friend never came at all. I felt sad and
abandoned.

My seventh friend came and held my hand and
said, '*I care. I'm here. I want to help you through this.*'
He stayed and I felt loved.

Those who stay and share in suffering are jewels beyond
price. For them the path is full of distress and sadness of a
different kind. To see your own child suffer is to have
your heart pierced by a sword. Any parent knows that, but
even those 'professional carers' face grief and despair as
those they have come to love struggle to persevere through
the pain. Georgie's nurse, Beverley, from the Ellenor
Foundation, gave me the following description (adapted
from *Lord, Let Me Love* by Marjorie Holmes) of what it
meant to her to watch constant suffering:

Oh God, this suffering . . . to be a helpless witness
to another person's suffering. It seems that my own I
could bear more easily. At least I could cry out

lustily, bloodily. I could wrestle it, fight it, put up a mighty battle.

But this. To be whole and strong, every sense vivid and vulnerable, to be called to attend a loved one's agony. To hear the cries and witness the struggle yet be powerless to put an end to it. Or to have to be brave because the sufferer is so brave. To be cheerful when the heart is breaking. To live within sight and sound and touch of the endless suffering. To be essential to the victim's very existence.

I cry out against this sometimes, Lord, even as I beg deliverance for the sufferer, or that some of these torments might be put upon me instead. Why do you allow it? What earthly good is such suffering? And why have I been cast in this role?

Then I realise that you are not the author of suffering, but that you alone can take our suffering and turn it to some good purpose. What that purpose is, I don't know, only that in it all you can only act out of love and for blessing. I hold on to that when everything around us suggests we are forgotten.

Surely for that reason you made me unusually strong, resilient, enduring. Able to comfort if only by not breaking down.

Lord, when I think I can endure this no longer, let me remember those who did not flee the scene of the cross. Help me keep my vigil with suffering as courageously as they kept theirs.

Courage. The vital thread in the complex tapestry of perseverance and endurance. There's no getting away from it and I wish it could be otherwise, but as with Bunyan's Christian in *A Pilgrim's Progress*, only a brave heart can overcome the giants of despair and lead our feet out of the slough of despond. As I have already mentioned, I don't mean the flashes of extraordinary heroism, the feats of astounding bravery which earned men and women medals and fame in world wars, but rather the steady tread of the thousands who witnessed all that they knew and loved being destroyed around them, all sense and hope disintegrating in cordite and shrapnel and yet still kept walking. 'Though he slay me, yet will I hope in him.'

In suffering we may feel overwhelmed by the persistence, the scale or the number of our problems. The Bible resounds with the anguished cries of those whose foes and troubles encompass them and their hearts faint within them. But time and again, we read that tiny word: 'yet'.

> Though the fig-tree does not bud
> and there be no grapes on the vines,
> though the olive crop fails
> and the fields produce no food,
> though there are no sheep in the pen
> and no cattle in the stalls,
> *yet* will I rejoice in the Lord,
> I will be joyful in God my Saviour.
> The Sovereign Lord is my strength.
> Habbakuk 3:17–19

In the same breath as the psalmist groans, 'O my God, I cry out by day, but you do not answer, by night, and am not silent', he gasps out defiantly:

> Yet you are enthroned as the Holy One;
> you are the praise of Israel.
> In you our fathers put their trust;
> they trusted and you delivered them.
> They cried to you and were saved;
> in you they trusted and were not disappointed.
>
> Psalm 22:2–5

In this book I have been telling Georgie's story, and as it is by no means over yet, it would be inappropriate to say 'she's completely better and we all lived happily ever after!' It is ongoing. Some days are good, some difficult. Many are a struggle with the debilitating headaches and constant fatigue spoiling her plans. But as with all journeys, you have to begin with *one step*. We are learning to do this by enjoying what we have *today*, what we can manage *today*, being thankful that we *have* today. But the account of Georgie's story is, inevitably, not only the tale of our journey as a family and as individuals, but also that of every 'bruised reed and smouldering wick'. Isn't it the story of us all? Few of us will avoid pain and difficulties. Many of us might be spared physical suffering but may find that happiness and fulfilment in our relationships elude us. It is often perplexing how marriages and friendships can totally disintegrate, why couples longing to have children are unable to conceive, how babies die in their sleep, a regular journey to work can turn into a tragedy with a road accident or train crash, how a routine operation ends in lifelong disability. We cannot live in perpetual sunlight. One of the few certainties of life is that darkness will overshadow us all in some way, at some time. And in due course, death itself will cover our earthly body, ending the battle which wins for us the precious prize for our perseverance – a crown of life. We pray that we will endure. We throw ourselves on God's grace and mercy, hoping and trusting that even if our heart breaks, our faith won't. We can only hold tightly onto the promise that God can heal the broken-hearted, and that we have a hope beyond the pain:

> We are hard pressed on every side, but not crushed; perplexed, but not in despair; persecuted, but not abandoned; struck down but not destroyed . . . Therefore we do not lose heart. Though outwardly we are wasting away, yet inwardly we are being renewed day by day. For our light and momentary troubles are achieving for us an eternal glory that far outweighs them all. So we fix our eyes not on what is seen but on what is unseen.
>
> 2 Corinthians 4:8–9, 16–18

Looking back occasionally can be helpful just to see how far we have actually come. When we were thinking about the cover for this book, I was keen to find a long flight of steps to depict the theme of taking one step, and one day, at a time, 'fixing our eyes not on what is seen but on what is unseen'. We finally found just the right steps at Aylesford Priory and spent a very hot but happy morning trying to get the right photograph. I walked up and down those steps a great number of times! But the photograph looking backwards, showing the endless steps continuing upwards, is really how I would like to finish this book. There are still many steps to climb, each one with their own story, but we *have* come a long way. As I glance backwards, it's not to say, 'If only', or 'I wish', but to remember something I was told by the chaplain at Burrswood: 'Rest in God's presence . . . Don't pull away . . . Wait . . . *Even empty shells can be useful.*'

And as I pause on this particular step, it's not to despair or to wallow in self-pity, but to picture *how* an empty shell could be useful. Then I realise. How free, how glorious, how childlike, to hear the sea when you put your ear to the shell!

Strong and deep love of Jesus, come in like the sea at high tide. Cover all my powers, drown all my sins, wash all my cares, lift up my earthbound soul and float it to my Lord's feet.

There let me lie, a poor broken shell, washed up by His love, having no virtue or value of my own. Only this I venture: to whisper to Him, that if He will put His ear to me, He will hear within my heart the faint echoes of the vast waves of His own love, love that has brought me where I delight to be: at His feet forever.

Charles Spurgeon

Addresses for Further Information

1. **The Oratory of the Little Way**
   P.O. Box 221
   Gaylordsville, Connecticut 06755, USA
   Tel.: 860 354 8294
   E-mail: HEAL2@aol.com
   Website: www.cysol.com/oratory

My brother, Nigel Mumford, is Director of the Oratory of the Little Way in Gaylordsville, Connecticut. Nigel served for six and a half years in Her Majesty's Royal Marine Commandos, two of which he spent as a drill instructor at the commando training school.

'Having been a drill instructor in the Royal Marine Commandos it was my job to teach recruits to kill or be killed. It is now a privilege to teach people to heal and be healed,' says Nigel. 'My primary mission now is to put people in touch with Christ the healer.'

The Oratory of the Little Way is an eight-bed retreat house with a chapel, where guests can go for an hour, a day, overnight or longer. The pace is relaxed. Guests are cared for in a quiet, gentle and loving environment where it is safe to be with God as healing takes place. Peace becomes the heavenly anaesthetic so God may heal as guests become de-stressed and ready to receive. The ministry is based on the foundation of the love and compassion of Jesus Christ.

Founded in 1965 by Father Benjamin Priest, and under the auspices of the Connecticut Diocese of the Episcopal Church, the Oratory is ecumenical, welcoming people from all denominations. Nigel Mumford is a Lay Minister, licensed by the Bishop for the healing ministry.

2. The Children's Ambulance/Kent Leukaemia and Cancer Equipment Fund
Peggy Wood MBE
5 Crompton Gardens
Off Hastings Road
Maidstone
Kent ME15 7HD
Tel.: 01622 756 641
Registered Charity No. 282944

Set up in 1980 by Peggy Wood, this charity became registered in April 1981. The Children's Ambulance was bought and equipped by the charity in January 1993 and provides an invaluable twenty-four-hour service taking Kent children with cancer to and from hospital. The service is completely funded by voluntary donations and is in constant demand.

3. The Ellenor Foundation
East Hill
Dartford
Kent DA1 1SA
Tel.: 01322 221315
Fax.: 01322 626503
Registered Charity No. 291870

The Ellenor Foundation is a Christian hospice charity that provides care free of charge to people of all faiths and none. It was set up in 1985 to provide care for patients of all ages living with cancer and other life-threatening illness, together with support for their families and friends. The charity provides a specialist service to children and, in the main, this enables families to remain together in their own homes. The paediatric nurses offer twenty-four-hour cover, and give support and reassurance to those caring for very sick children alongside any medical treatment that is needed. Respite care is also available.

4. Burrswood
Groombridge
Tunbridge Wells
Kent TN3 9PY
Tel.: 01892 863 637
Fax.: 01892 863 623
E-mail: admin@burrswood.org.uk
Website: www.burrswood.org.uk
Registered Charity No. 229261

JULIE SHELDON

Burrswood was established as a Christian healing centre in 1948 by the late Dorothy Kerin. Over fifty years later the team at Burrswood have pioneered a most effective model of interdisciplinary Christian 'whole person' care. The hospital unit enables this team to deliver the best of professional care in this unique place. The Church of Christ the Healer is at the centre of the work with the aim being to keep the love of Christ at the heart of care. While it is a Christian community, people of other faiths and convictions are welcome. There are four healing services each week which are open to the public.